COUNTRY & WESTERN AMERICANA

George W. Northrup, a Minnesota frontiersman,
posing with the tools of a gold miner.
Minnesota Historical Society, St Paul.

COLLECTING
COUNTRY & WESTERN
AMERICANA
DOREEN BECK

BELMONT SALOON.

HAMLYN
London · New York · Sydney · Toronto

endpapers
Quilted patchwork coverlet, Baltimore, about
1850. The American Museum in Britain, Bath.

title page
A mule train arrives in Helena, Montana, in
1874. Montana Historical Society, Helena.

Published by
The Hamlyn Publishing Group Limited
London · New York · Sydney, Toronto
Astronaut House, Feltham, Middlesex, England
© Copyright The Hamlyn Publishing Group Limited 1975

ISBN 0 600 37043 7

Filmset in England by
Keyspools Limited, Golborne, Lancashire

Printed in Hong Kong by
Toppan Printing Co., (H.K.) Ltd.

Introduction

H OW can you collect all that worthless American stuff when you've been brought up on Rembrandts and Monets?

In one form or another this question must have been asked of all the crazy people—a handful of curious, stubborn and far-seeing collectors—who, in the late decades of the 19th century and the early decades of this one, first discovered and appreciated Americana.

Today, crowds flock to see the treasures from those pioneering collections, now more often than not enshrined in one or other of the country's major institutions. More and more Americans are discovering the charms of their own past, and the whole country, once noted for its hot pursuit of progress and change, seems to have turned antiquarian, nostalgic, even sentimental, is looking backwards, searching for roots, has, in two words, Americana fever. (The young talking of 'antiquing' their blue jeans, when they bleach the colour out of them, is one of the more bizarre symptoms of the disease, although, perhaps it is not so bizarre, if you can believe the stories of cowboys sitting in watering troughs in order to shrink their denim dungarees into a skin-tight fit as a protection against saddlesores, among other afflictions. That old *serge de Nîmes* is very accommodating!)

Maybe Thomas Jefferson, more than a century ago,

1. Nels Wickstrom, a true settler and pioneer from Florence County, posing with his family for an unknown photographer in 1893. In wooded states like Wisconsin you built your house with logs like Nels did. State Historical Society of Wisconsin, Madison, Florence Collection, 1893.

6

2. Some experts have noted the natural, everyday quality in this portrait of Paul Revere, silversmith, by one of the country's earliest and best self-taught artists, John Singleton Copley. Others point to the duality of art and craft, the interplay of head and hand, and suggest that the dominance of the craftsman's head in the painting shows that the painter believed in the primacy of conception or art over technical skill or craft. In 1767 Copley complained bitterly about Boston's attitude to his art: 'The people generally regard it as no more than any other useful trade, as they sometimes term it, like that of a Carpenter or shew maker, not as one of the most noble Arts in the World'. Just where that fine line should be drawn in much of what is now called Americana still remains to be decided. Museum of Fine Arts, Boston, Massachusetts. Gift of Joseph W., William B. and Edward H. R. Revere.

3. A little bit of Old England. Windsor chairs were first made on this side of the Atlantic in the late 1720s in the Philadelphia area and subsequently developed distinctive characteristics in New England and Pennsylvania. The writing-arm Windsor is uniquely American. There is widespread evidence of the popularity of Windsor chairs here, even in sophisticated circles – those 18th-century gentlemen who met to plot and plan revolution in Philadelphia in the 1770s sat around in Windsors. One of them, Roger Sherman, the shoemaker from Connecticut, is just visible at left sitting in the earliest low-back type in the portrait painted of him by Ralph Earl. Furniture-making was one of the foremost crafts of the Colonial 18th century. Yale University Art Gallery, New Haven, Connecticut.

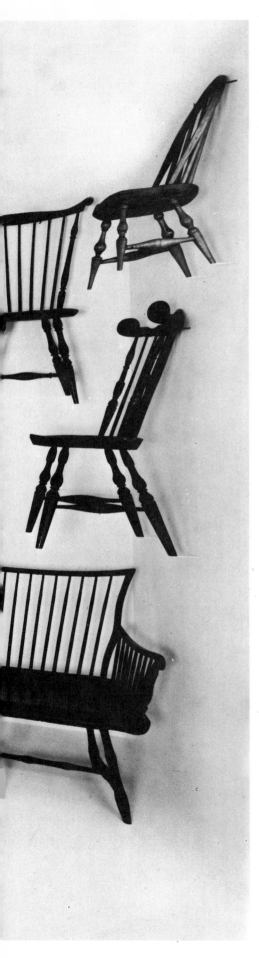

saw the way it would be, when he said of the writing-box on which he wrote the Declaration of Independence, 'It claims no merit of particular beauty. It is plain, neat, convenient . . . it yet displays itself sufficiently for any writing. . . . Its imaginary value will increase with years . . . [and it will] be carried in the procession of our nation's birthday as the relics of saints are in those of the Church'. He could scarcely have anticipated how many different kinds of relics his fellow citizens would go looking for, or how many saints—anonymous and otherwise—besides himself they would make!

The word 'Americana' is, of course, a Latin adjective, but its use was already limited to the northern part of the continents named after Amerigo Vespucci in at least one book published in London in the latter part of the 18th century, the now extremely rare, *Scenographia Americana*, which contains 'A collection of views in North America and the West Indies neatly engraved from drawings taken on the spot by members of the Army and Navy'. Its use was further limited to the United States, a name impossible to turn into an adjective in any language that I know of, when in the early part of the 19th century, following in the wake of the *Encyclopedia Britannica*, the first encyclopedia to be published on these shores was named the *Encyclopedia Americana*. It was no more limited to things American than the *Encyclopedia Britannica* had been limited to things British. They both treated of nothing less than the whole of human knowledge, the adjective in this case merely referring to the place where the whole enterprise was conceived.

At what moment in time the Latin adjective came into common use as an American noun, is difficult to establish. Noah Webster did not define it in the original edition of his *American Dictionary of the English Language*, which was published in 1828, and its existence was not recognised by his successors until the third major revision of his work appeared almost a century later, in 1909, under a new title, *Webster's New International Dictionary of the English Language*. The definition was then briefly given as 'literary, ethnographical, historical or other matters relating to America'. Emphasis was not given to objects and culture until the third edition of the *New International* appeared in 1961. The ethnographical element was then dropped and the word defined as 'materials (as literary or historical documents and relics) distinctly bearing on, concerning or characteristic of America, its civilization or its culture'. The word still does not rate a full entry in the *Oxford English Dictionary*, but then that venerable work has not yet taken note of the widespread extension, if not total shift, in the meaning of words with an -ana ending! In current usage, such words as Americana, as well as Victoriana and Canadiana, have more to do with relics and objects than with sayings and anecdotes, in the old sense. There are

REAPING MACHINES.

Plate XXXV.

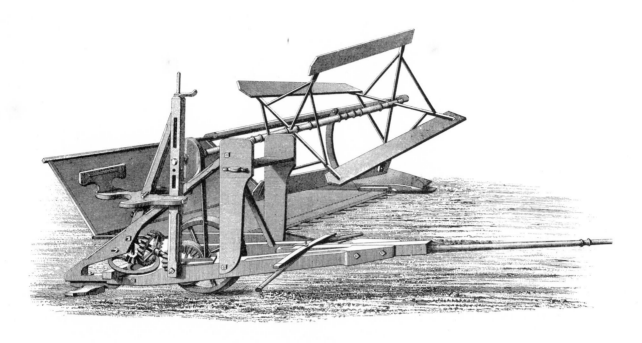

M^c CORMICK'S AMERICAN REAPER.

$\frac{1}{36}$ of the full size

Henry Stone del.^t

HUSSEY'S AMERICAN REAPER

J.W. Lowry fc

$\frac{1}{36}$ of the full size.

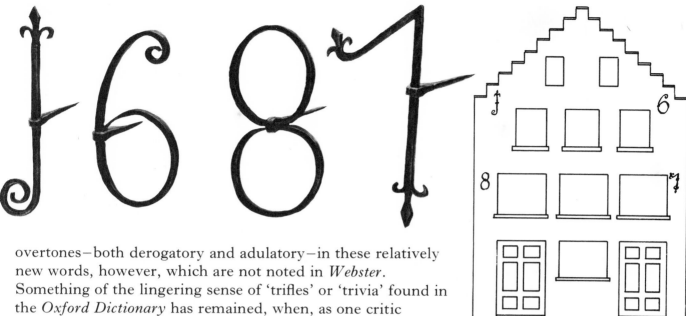

overtones—both derogatory and adulatory—in these relatively new words, however, which are not noted in *Webster*. Something of the lingering sense of 'trifles' or 'trivia' found in the *Oxford Dictionary* has remained, when, as one critic points out, the paintings of men such as Eastman Johnson were once regarded as 'mere Americana'. But today those same paintings are regarded as 'valuable Americana', and the word has taken on a reverent overtone. It has, as you might guess, been picked up by Madison Avenue and dealers both scrupulous and unscrupulous. Even manufacturers of paper handkerchiefs attach it to their product which they package—rather attractively, it must be said—in boxes decorated with the stitches of early 19th-century samplers for the ladies, and with the American eagle for the gentlemen.

Whole industries are, in fact, feeding off the nostalgia boom, and pewter sculptures and commemorative plates and the like are getting to be a habit. With the bicentennial of the country's birth in 1776 already in the air, everyone is trying to remember. Major exhibitions, including one for London's Victoria and Albert Museum in the bicentennial year itself, are being staged or planned to help them do so. The Post Office has got into the habit of issuing sets of stamps that tell a story about the country's past. In 1972 a series was issued commemorating the crafts practised in these parts, mostly in Colonial times, and in 1973 a series was devoted to the Rise of the Spirit of Independence. Several States have announced their intention of issuing official medals commemorating the part they played in winning the War of Independence against you-know-who. A naturalised citizen, Amerigo Giannicchi, perhaps appropriately enough, won New York's statewide contest for his design.

Among the flood of reproductions made at the time of the centennial celebrations in 1876 were several of the writing-box mentioned earlier, on which Jefferson wrote the Declaration of Independence. As the years went by, each owner of a replica thought his of hers was the original. Even the replica once owned by the German Chancellor Bismarck

4. Above: McCormick's American reaper; below: Hussey's American reaper. From the *Popular Encyclopedia or Conversations Lexicon*, published by Blackie & Son in about 1865.

5. A little bit of Old Holland. Wrought iron figures from the façade of the Old Tile House in New Castle, Delaware. The fact that the colony was under English rule by 1687 did not deter the original Dutch owner from building a house like the one he had always wanted in the Old Country, perhaps at the time when he had the means or the leisure to do so.

was for a time mistaken for the original, and is now safely ensconced in the Smithsonian Institution in Washington. Milling marks on the metal of what were thought to be George Washington inaugural buttons established the fact that they, too, had been made in the 1870s.

The better reproductions made nowadays are limited, numbered and registered, so that they can always be identified as reproductions. But others are made to seem much more than they are. They are fakes, in a word, and they have always been, and probably always will be, part of the human scene. James Fenimore Cooper, America's first important novelist, noted that counterfeiters were busy in the woods of New York State in the early years of the 19th century, circulating base coin from one end of the Union to the other. Not a few early engravers are known to have been tempted to misuse their skills. Copies of attractive glass whisky flasks, made and sold quite cheaply only a few years ago, have recently been mistakenly identified as originals made—when the best ones were—in the first half of the 19th century. A Hobby Protection

6. A little bit of Old Spain. A painted wooden *bulto* or figure in the round of Saint Santiago made by an unknown perhaps itinerant artist thought to have been working in the Chimayo area of what is now New Mexico in the early part of the 19th century. Saint Santiago is, appropriately enough for an area so dependent on horses, the patron saint of that animal and its riders. Just which of the numerous James Saints he grew out of I have not been able to determine.

7. The eagle as hitching post—a cast iron model made in 1870 at the Pioneer Iron Works in San Francisco, California.

8. The eagle and the flag in a 19th-century hooked rug thought to have been made in New Hampshire.

Act, which became law in November 1973, is meant to ensure that all reproductions of coins and political items are adequately marked as such, either with the word 'copy' clearly marked on them, or the date of manufacture.

Obsessed as we are with the pressures of supply and demand economics, it should come as a surprise to no one that the nostalgia boom has, in addition, led to a skyrocketing of prices for old and not so old things. These are surpassed only by the prices paid for examples of modern American painting and sculpture—which no one ever calls Americana, of course, perhaps because in their case artistry is considered to have triumphed over mere historical interest!

Worldwide demand for examples of modern American painting and sculpture forced the price of a painting by Jackson Pollock called *Blue Poles* up to an incredible all-time record of $2 million in 1972. (One of the more delicious ironies of that transaction is that the artist used house-paint for his creation, so it is going to crumble apart ere long, unless science comes up with some new method for preserving

it!) Only a little less demand forced the price of a painted tin candlebox up to $10,000 about the same time. It was charming, a good and rare example of the work of an anonymous Pennsylvania craftsman, probably in the late 18th century. But whether it is worth what amounts to a year's salary for a great many people, even in the United States, is debatable.

Since the stock market is shaky, currency rates up and down and inflation rampant, rare and unique objects have become, as one critic has noted, 'the trading beads of the jet set', not to mention other lesser mortals trying to keep their heads above water. Collectors are scrambling to revise their insurance evaluations sharply upwards and there are mutterings that folk art—or whatever term you like to apply to the various arts and crafts now lumped under that heading—is no longer for the folk, but for wealthy collectors and dealers, investors and institutions, local and foreign.

I grieve that the original creators get no share in this instant profit-taking. I can only hope they received a fair price for their labour in the first place. But I am shocked when I hear that examples of glassware once rejected as seconds now fetch higher prices than perfect examples of the same ware, merely because the former are rare and the latter plentiful. This is the error in the stamp syndrome, or supply and demand gone berserk! I have not yet devised a system for correcting any of these inequities. I'm hoping an economist will do it for me some time soon.

I am not, however, in total sympathy with the museum personnel who complain that the public only wants to see the piece that cost them $60,000 or $100,000 and spends more time speculating on how much a piece cost rather than on considering its intrinsic worth. After all, a healthy—or maybe unhealthy—dollop of the public's tax dollars and/or blood, sweat and tears probably helped pay, either directly or indirectly, for the Pollock, the rare highboy, the tin candlebox, or whatever. As at least one cynical observer has noted, many of the major restorations—houses, villages (a whole town in the case of Williamsburg, Virginia), restored to the way they looked at some stage during the last three or four centuries—now dotting the land, were financed wholly, or in part, by the Henry Fords, John D. Rockefellers and Henry Francis du Ponts of this world, men who might very well have felt that they had debts to repay, and that one way of repaying them was to buy back a past they had so successfully and so rapidly changed. Moreover, since museums continue to give us visual indigestion by displaying too many similar objects together—witness the British Museum's room upon room of Greek vases and the Shelburne Museum's case upon case of wooden decoys—knowing that one piece cost ten or a hundred times more than the others, helps refocus attention, if not wrath, wondrously well.

9. A little bit of Old Germany. Two handsome wooden butter moulds showing variations on the tulip design characteristic of much Pennsylvania German design. The German immigrant craftsmen to Pennsylvania were among the most skilful of all those who came to these shores in search of freedom, fame and fortune.

Foreign interest in American art and artifacts is a relatively new phenomenon. An exhibition entitled 'American Naive Painting of the 18th and 19th Centuries' which consisted of '111 Masterpieces from the collection of Edgar William and Bernice Chrysler Garbisch' and was seen in several European cities in 1968 and 1969 (as well as in Canada and various parts of the United States), is said to have helped change the image of America's past in Europe. A large exhibition of 19th-century American quilts is presently on an international tour and is scheduled to go even to Russia as part of the programme of cultural exchange. Cultural exchange is one thing most Americans would not object to, but foreign ownership of American art and artifacts is quite another, and many Americans are not too happy about that at all! Now there's a switch! For years, Americans have been the owners

10. The eagle in the hands of an itinerant carver, Wilhelm Schimmel, who roamed the Pennsylvania countryside in the post Civil War years, whittling birds and animals in return for room and board and rum. Schimmel is now considered to be one of the most notable American folk sculptors but he never bothered to sign the more than five hundred pieces now attributed to him on the basis of stylistic similarities.

11. Spinning wheel found in an attic in Haverstraw on the Hudson river, 1830. Girls used to carry wheels like this one to spinning parties, where they would spin wool or flax. The American Museum in Britain, Bath.

of some of the world's most renowned art treasures. But now that a designer in Rome is selling American quilts, and English and French dealers are competing with Americans in scouring the countryside from Pennsylvania to Oklahoma and Hawaii in search of the same objects, not to mention the numerous and much publicised foreign purchases of modern American paintings and sculptures, many Americans are up in arms and argue that the time has come for a National Treasures Act to prohibit the export of such things. But other, perhaps more philosophical voices, say, 'Why not send our art abroad, as long as we keep the best pieces here at home?'. It looks as though it will be an ongoing debate, as the saying goes, for some time to come.

By the time I was walking under the covered bridge that led me, this summer, into the grounds of an American

12. A simple quilt design, which because of its two opposing names nicely symbolises Country and Western Americana: Turkey Tracks—for those who stayed home and minded the farm or the store or whatever; and Wandering Foot—for those who went west. Alas, the design is also known by a third, more sombre name, 'Death's Black Darts'—which just goes to show how difficult it sometimes is to make hard and fast distinctions!

13. The eagle in peril—a Civil War drum which belonged to the Ninth Regiment of Vermont Volunteers, one of the first volunteer regiments to be mustered in support of the Northern or Union side. Tennessee, one of the last States to secede from the Union, is, perhaps ironically enough, known as the Volunteer State.

past re-created on 45 acres of land at Shelburne, Vermont, and was lingering in Conkey's Tavern, 3,000 miles away across the Atlantic, I was thinking seriously about Americana fever. Conkey's Tavern and the buildings that make up the Shelburne Museum have been restored to the way they looked at some stage during the last two or three centuries. The Tavern, in addition, has been transplanted, in a sense returned home, from its native village in Massachusetts to English soil, or more precisely, to an elegant mansion near Bath, Somerset, where the first American Museum outside of the United States has been installed. Had I walked into some strange surrealistic cemeteries? Was Americana fever a disease, a local variant of antique fever which is tending to epidemic proportions in practically all parts of the world, or was it a vital attempt to come to grips with the past? Was it sheer arrogance to call all that American stuff worthless, and sheer nonsense to set it all indiscriminately with high price tags on pedestals labelled 'Americana'?

The pioneer collectors of things American concentrated on the work of relatively sophisticated craftsmen such as furniture-makers and silversmiths—whipped cream Americana, as it were—which was produced mainly during the Colonial period and mainly in the north-eastern States from Maine to Pennsylvania until about 1820–30. The cut-off point for fine, locally-made pieces, which gradually came to include examples from the other decorative arts such as glassware, textiles, pewterware, and treen (made from trees or woodware, if you will), was set around 1820–30 because the wild and ebullient mixing of styles that characterised many of the decorative arts after that time, along with what was considered the ominous arrival of mass-production, was thought to be beyond the attention of all self-respecting aesthetes.

In 1970, an exhibition on 19th-century America at New York's Metropolitan Museum made the 19th century a little

14. The minutemen of Bridgehampton, Long Island, embroidered on the valance of a homespun linen bed curtain about 1776. The minutemen were farmers, grocers, coopers, bakers – ready to seize arms at a moment's notice. Paul Revere, the sitter in Copley's portrait, is almost as famous for his equestrian feats as for his silversmithing. In 1775 he rode hot pace through the night from Boston to Lexington and Concord to warn the minutemen of those towns that the British were coming.

more respectable, but it too concentrated on the whipped cream, the work of relatively sophisticated craftsmen, sometimes working with mass-production methods, and of academically trained painters and sculptors.

Even way back in the 1930s, however, interest in what New York's Museum of Modern Art called 'the art of the common man' had been spreading, and it began to seem that weathervanes and cigarstore Indians, figureheads and whirligigs and painted signs and primitive pictures had more native vigour, a more strictly American quality than whipped cream Americana, much of which was essentially derived from English and French designs. No less an observer than the 20th-century artistic virtuoso, Pablo Picasso, once remarked: 'Cocks have always been seen, but never as well as in American weathervanes.'

In the late 1930s, in an inspired attempt not just to put to work unemployed artists, but also to go some way towards meeting the growing demand for pictorial information about American design and craftsmanship, the Federal Government undertook to compile the Index of American Design. The objects recorded in watercolours in the Index, now stored in Washington's National Gallery, were selected on the basis of artistic and historic significance and were made by predominantly European immigrants and their children and their children's children. The art of the common man – and woman – is found there side by side with that of more sophisticated craftsmen – and women – and with what one observer has called 'the lower levels of useful workmanship' and which I prefer to call bread-and-butter Americana, the until recently neglected tools and utensils of fields and mines, homes and taverns, the numerous objects which help to illustrate the daily life of another age, and which can have a certain abstract beauty, even when their original use is no longer known.

But despite all these efforts, the study of the arts and crafts practised on these shores is still in its infancy and strict categories and definitions have not yet been devised for their orderly consideration. Just when, for example, Americana can be elevated from the realm of History into the more rarified spheres of Art, remains problematical. The Smithsonian Institution in Washington chooses to house its collections of things American in its Museum of History & Technology, Yale University in its Art Gallery. Both bring and hope to extend their collections up to the present time, the former concentrating on the technological, the latter on what used to be called the Great Arts of painting and sculpture and the Minor or Decorative Arts, or just about everything else! Critics and cultural historians as well as antique dealers, try as they might, have not been able to come up with good generic labels, particularly for the work of the less sophisticated

15. Hand blown, olive amber, shoe blacking bottle of the early 19th century.

16. Pablo Picasso, artistic virtuoso of the 20th century, once said, 'Cocks have always been seen but never as well as in American weathervanes'. This gilded copper example from a Massachusetts church steeple was made by America's first documented weathervane-maker–Shem Drowne of Boston–in the early part of the 18th century.

17. The ubiquitous eagle–proud symbol of the new Republic created in 1776 and found long afterwards in carvings and tavern signs, on furniture and textiles, pewter and tin, sashes and fans, buttons and bows. This one may or may not have been made by John Bellamy, a ship's carver from Maine, who became famous for his eagles and for what one expert calls his knack of reducing the bird's anatomy to a 'decorative shorthand'. But he had many imitators, and another expert sees Bellamy's hand here only in the carving of the beak!

23

craftsmen, artisans and artists. They use such terms as folk
art, pioneer, popular, primitive, naive, native, rural or
vernacular art, and, most recently, industrial art. But none of
these terms alone is wholly satisfactory and so, for the time
being, Americana will have to do. It has a pleasant ring and
an all-embracing, even if amorphous meaning.

Although the majority of collectors would probably
emphasise the 'made in America' aspect of Americana, in
accordance with Webster's definition, a case can be made for
including some of the things not necessarily made but certainly
widely used in this part of the world. *The Concise Encyclopedia
of American Antiques* does, in fact, include sections on 'the
oriental carpitt in colonial America', the ubiquitous China
trade porcelain, and such British pottery as spatterware and
the two Gaudies—Welsh and Dutch—which were made for the
American market, as were the German locks to be seen in a
display of ironware in Yale University Art Gallery's American
Wing, which is now called 'American Arts & the American
Experience'. I would like to include, in passing, a silver gorget,
thought to have been made in Montreal and given as a gift to
an Indian chief at Fort Berthold, North Dakota, where it was

24

excavated, and the strings and strings of beads used in trade with the Indians and made who knows where. I like the thought of red Manchester cloth, made in English factories in the early part of the 19th century, turning up as the lining for leggings made in New Mexico, and I am intrigued by a description of goods seen at the International Exhibition in Paris in 1867 and labelled, '*Qualité extra-sublime. Fabriqué spécialement pour l'Amérique*'. (Extra sublime quality. Made especially for America.)

As you can perhaps begin to realise, defining what is American is almost as difficult as defining what is un-American. Wandering around in the backstreets of New York recently, I discovered a small dealer who had obviously given up on fine distinctions. His shop sign said, 'Historical Americana', but he was actually dealing in English, German and Russian military relics, as well as in American Civil War buttons!

The *Oxford Companion to Art* says William Sidney Mount's painting, *Long Island Farm*, executed in about 1854, 'is as American as pumpkin pie'. But my cook book tells me that pumpkin pie used to be very Old English. And it is, in fact, tempting to define Americana as recollections of Old

18 & 19. Glass, like furniture and silver, is in the whipped cream category of Americana that has been much written about, but I couldn't resist including these two examples here, the jug because it is thought to be peculiarly American in its decoration, and the bottle because it is a lovely thing and was made in Ohio in the early part of the 19th century at a time when that area was on the edge of the wilderness.

20. The Conestoga Wagon–a uniquely American creation developed by primarily German immigrant craftsmen in the hinterland of Philadelphia on what one expert calls 'the hither edge of civilization' in the middle of the 18th century. Pulled by teams of six specially bred horses and travelling in convoys of a hundred or more, these huge freight trains became a familiar sight along the wagon roads leading from Lancaster to Philadelphia in the East, Pittsburgh in the West and the Yadkin in the South. An astonished Scottish immigrant who had never seen anything like it in the Old Country gazed in wonder on what he called 'these huge moving houses'. **The American Museum in Britain, Bath.**

21. Conkey's Tavern which was built by William Conkey in 1753 was transported from Pelham, Massachusetts, to the American Museum in Britain, Bath, where it can now be visited. The American Museum in Britain, Bath.

22. Indian weathervane of polychromed sheet iron from the latter part of the 19th century. Some of the earliest European settlers are said to have placed Indian weathervanes on their roof-tops as symbols of friendship towards the original inhabitants of this continent. The ethnographic element found in the definition of Americana in the early 20th-century editions of *Webster's English Dictionary* has been dropped from the current edition. The Indians' story is too vast and special to be included here except occasionally as graphic figures.

England, mostly, but also of Old Spain, Old Germany, Old Holland, Old France, Old China, to name only a few of the principal ingredients that went into the making of America. Many a piece of furniture pronounced American or English has turned out to be just the opposite, and there is actually no foolproof way of telling where an unmarked piece of ironware or a printed textile, or a pewter plate actually came from. In the case of a plain, unmarked pewter plate, it was more than likely made on these shores from some battered imported piece or pieces melted down and reworked. In the case of one painted chest, Old Spain seems to have been eliminated from the argument, but there is no certainty as to whether the piece was made and decorated in what is now New Mexico or whether it was made and decorated south of the border in Old Mexico!

There is some historical justification for simply defining Americana as all the things the British banned the original thirteen colonies from making, but which they, or at least those north of the Mason-Dixon line separating Pennsylvania from Virginia, went ahead in their stubbornly independent way and made all the same. The attitude of the British Government is well summed up in a letter to the Governor of New Hampshire in 1743: 'It is our express Will and Pleasure that you do not upon any Pretense whatever give your consent to a Law or Laws for setting up manufactures which are hurtful or prejudicial to this kingdom'. But as early as 1733, a royal commissioner had noted . . . 'the People of New England, being obliged to apply themselves to manufactures more than others of the Plantations who have Benefit of a better soil and warmer Climate [have made] such improvements . . . lately . . . in all sorts of Mechanic Arts that not only Scrutores, Chairs and other Wooden Manufactures, but Hoes, axes and other Iron utensils are now exported . . . to the other Plantations, which if not prevented may be of ill consequence to the Trade and Manufacture of this Kingdom, which Evil may be worthy of the consideration of a British Parliament'. We all know how right His Majesty's Commissioner was!

Long after Independence, the north-eastern States from Maine to Pennsylvania remained the 'manufacturing' heartland of the United States, trading not just with the South but increasingly with the interior. In the early part of the 19th century, an enterprising businessman from Connecticut, called Lambert Hitchcock, was scouting out the possibilities for selling his painted furniture 'in the village of Chicago'. The guns that won the West were for the most part made in the north east. The reapers that conquered the Mid-West, 'the smooth, lawn-like surface of the prairie' as a Scottish visitor described it, untouched by any plowshare, were first mass-produced in 1846—only 100 to start with—in a factory in New York State under license from the inventor, Cyrus

23. The country store—once the centre of a good deal of social, not to mention economic activity—now preserved as a museum in Fredericksburg, Virginia. The building dates from 1796 and has been stocked with items mostly dating from the post Civil War period found in the Fredericksburg area by a life-long collector, D. Letcher Stoner. The wagon just visible at right, sometimes called a drummer's wagon, was used by itinerant salesmen visiting farms and settlements in the back country.

24. Log cabin quilt of about 1890. The characteristic design of the American frontier home, at least in wooded areas, adapted to quilt-making was an economical way of using up even the smallest fragments of material. A surprising variety of designs was achieved by manipulating the width of the strips and the placement of the various colours. This s a variation on the 'barn-raising' design.

25. Although Yale University Art Gallery has no record of how they acquired this head of Benjamin Franklin, there is some evidence that our dictionary-writing friend, Noah Webster, got it from the sculptor, William Rush of Philadelphia, and gave it to a friend who gave it to the Gallery. Rush is known for his ships' figureheads and other carvings in wood—a reason for some to quibble with his title as First American Sculptor!

McCormick. The man in a remote sawmill in California who saw the need for a saw with interchangeable teeth, because he was far from any repair shops, came back East to manufacture his invention. Barbed wire caused bitter fights between those who wanted to fence in the open range and those who did not. It also led to a few legal battles among the eastern manufacturers struggling to control some of the patents on it.

The more sophisticated craftsmen congregated in the bustling towns of the eastern seaboard such as Boston, Philadelphia, Newport and New York, and a little further south in Baltimore and Charleston, but numerous Yankee pedlars and other itinerant traders, whittlers and artists of one sort or another, roamed the countryside in search of business. And many a family making its pitch in the wilderness of New York State or Vermont, or further west into the Ohio Valley as far as the Mississippi and beyond it to the Great Plains and the Rockies and beyond them to California (some preferred to approach that El Dorado from the sea), had to shift for themselves just as the earliest, mainly European settlers along the eastern seaboard had done before them. According to James Fenimore Cooper, in his novel about upper New York State, *The Pioneers*, whole neighbourhoods in the Old States were tempted 'to enter those wild mountains in search of competence and happiness', to leave their farms in Connecticut and Massachusetts and, 'make a trial of fortune in the woods'. Many a youngster and an oldster had, in fact, already gone west before newspaperman and presidential hopeful, Horace Greely, coined his famous phrase, 'Go West, young man'.

In 1847, Francis Parkman noted in his book, *The Oregon Trail* . . . 'the shattered wrecks of ancient clawfooted tables, well waxed and rubbed or massive bureaux of carved oak . . . some . . . no doubt the relics of ancestral prosperity in the colonial time . . . brought perhaps originally from England; then with the declining fortunes of their owners, borne across the Alleghenies to the wilderness of Ohio or Kentucky; then to Illinois or Missouri; and now at last fondly stowed away in the family wagon for the interminable journey to Oregon. But the stern privations of the way are little anticipated. The cherished relic is soon flung out to scorch and crack upon the hot prairie.' Many a mining association off to California to mine gold, convert it into coin and return home wealthy, also found they had to jettison the heavy iron and steel coinage equipment—presses, rollers, dies—when the going got rough crossing the plains and mountains or the Isthmus of Panama. One young woman I heard of recently was understandably enchanted when she came upon a patchwork quilt in New Mexico that had been made in the 1860s in an area of New York where she herself was born. It had somehow survived the journey west.

26. The traditional Pennsylvania German hearts and tulips on a cast iron stove plate made by George Stevenson in 1763. Anglo-Americans are said to have stuck to their open fires longer than their German American compatriots.

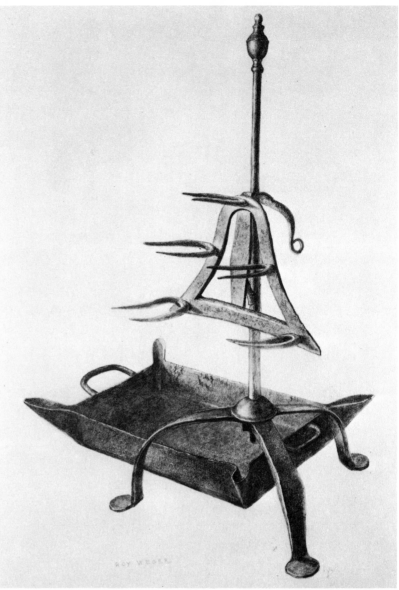

27. Wrought iron roasting stand and sheet metal drip pan with all four corners shaped for pouring, probably made in the 18th century.

Manufacturing centres began opening up in the Mid-West in and around the Mississippi Valley, particularly in Ohio in the early part of the 19th century, but the industrial development of more than half of the country lying west of the Mississippi, despite the gold and silver rushes to California as early as 1849 and to Colorado in 1859, did not take place until the early part of the 20th century, which is just about when the West, or more precisely, the frontier, is said to have disappeared. Historians differ on the exact date, but an easy one to take seems to be 1912, when Arizona and New Mexico, the last of the western territories, attained statehood.

Since hard and fast distinctions are not always easy to make, I am simply going to pick and choose from among all the objects loosely referred to as Americana, but particularly from among the bread-and-butter variety of those which are thought to have been made locally and which reveal something of the texture—and textures—of country living as the nation pushed westwards mainly during the 19th century.

Country wares

IN its review of Mrs Frances Trollope's rather carping study of American life published in 1832, *Domestic Manners of the Americans*, London's *Penny Magazine* wrote: 'In a new country where every man's hands are full of work, the useful most predominate over the ornamental. The things after which Mrs Trollope's heart yearned were dependent on the civilization of centuries, on the existence of a body wealthy and idle enough to be elegant in all things. These are circumstances which the Americans may be acquainted with in after years, but which they can no more create suddenly . . . than we could convert our cultivated fields and convenient streams into the sublimities of their primeval forests and mighty rivers'. Silver forks, in other words, are a needless extravagance when a horse or a farm implement is of greater necessity and worth.

That the useful did not altogether preclude the ornamental, however, is evident in numerous examples of bread-and-butter Americana as well as the more sophisticated whipped cream type. Whilst there is some evidence that the arts and crafts did deteriorate in Colonial times, particularly in rural areas, because of what is called 'the corrosive effect of the wilderness' on skilled craftsmen, by the latter half of the 18th century, the 'Buy American' campaigns of opposition to British policies had given a tremendous spurt to local woodworking and metal trades, for example.

28. The country store was a popular meeting place. The one illustrated here, in Pentwater, Michigan, photographed by Carrie Ellen Mears in about 1900, was typical. You could buy almost anything here: horseshoes, buggy tires or hurricane lamps. Chicago Historical Society, Illinois.

Today, in addition, the once scorned objects of mass-production are being looked at with new respect, not just as evidence of what one expert calls: 'the leap from Robinsonian conditions amid virgin forest to an advanced stage of mechanization', but as new forms that went hand in hand with new production methods. Implement after implement was re-shaped and differentiated for the more exacting American environment—the axe, the knife, the saw, the hammer, the shovel, household utensils and appliances that had remained static for centuries in Europe—and everybody seemed to be inventing something, seeking new ways to make goods more speedily, more perfectly and often of improved beauty. Even some of the drawings for the patents that flowed from this upsurge of inventiveness are said to have an artistic directness distinguishing them from the technical routine of a later age, and in the opinion of one expert, 'no small portion of folk art' lies concealed therein. By 1859, emigrants from Britain were being advised to take nothing with them but a trunkful of clothes, because they would find better tools in Illinois than in England.

There seem to be many reasons why Americans mechanised the complicated crafts, such as farming, from an early date and vigorously and intensively after about 1850—the dimensions of the West, the sparseness of the population, the lack of trained labour and the correspondingly high wages—but one expert also emphasises a less tangible reason, namely that immigrants, suddenly cut off from organised crafts and the whole culture in which such institutions had grown, were forced back on their imaginations in their efforts to come to grips with a new environment.

As early as 1838 a correspondent for a London magazine remarked: 'A man takes out a patent for the manufacture of some domestic article—a churn, for instance—and having stuck to his plane and his chisel until he has got as many made as a small waggon with one or two horses will conveniently carry, he immediately harnesses his team, and sets out without any definite plan for his journey, and "peddles" his churns from town to town and village to village, until he has managed to dispose of his cargo. So it is with all other minor manufactures; the manufacturer, instead of waiting for orders, sets off with a load of his merchandize, and does not return until he has converted it into money or goods of some sort that will answer his purpose equally well.'

The 'invent something and get rich quick' bee that was buzzing about the land was not without its casualties, of course. One of them, William Morton, an impecunious Massachusetts dentist, deserves our undying gratitude for his demonstration of the pain-killing effects of ether for tooth extraction in 1846. But the poor man spent his last years in futile, debt-ridden attempts to extract patent fees or disputed

29. A small pine hand loom made by a Shaker craftsman in the 19th century.

30. Embroidered homespun woollen bedspread made, according to family records, by the six sisters of the Honourable Amos Patterson of Washington Hall near Binghampton, New York, towards the end of the 18th century.

31. A friendship or album quilt – so named because the blocks and squares were made and donated by relatives and friends. This type of quilt-making was a veritable craze around the middle of the 19th century. The grand piecing together and appliquéing of the whole creation onto an unbleached muslin ground was an excuse for a festive social gathering.

Congressional appropriations for the substance he dubbed mysteriously 'letheon', but which was, in fact, nothing more than sulphuric ether.

The more famous patent models such as Samuel Morse's telegraphs patented between 1832 and 1846, Thomas Edison's first phonograph patented in 1877 and Graham Bell's original telephone transmitter and receiver of 1876, are now safely housed in the Smithsonian Institution in Washington, or in other museums such as the Henry Ford Museum at Dearborn, Michigan. But to the dismay of historians wanting to study the process of mechanisation, the Patent Office auctioned off all its other models with Congressional sanction when it needed space in the 1920s. Some of them were recently dug out of oblivion and put on display in roving exhibition/ sales in prestigious stores in New York, Dallas and Los Angeles, with price tags in the $125 to $1,150 range, and it begins to look as if these once neglected relics will be given house room by collectors now going after the guts and gadgetry of our early industrial civilisation.

Much work still remains to be done in this area, however, in sorting out the significant from the insignificant, the lasting innovation from the frivolous, but that should not stop us from joining in the guessing games that one collector friend of mine likes to play with the Things in his Den of Antiquity, some of whose weird and wonderful functions are matched only by their weird and wonderful names. Roll firkins and piggins around your tongue, and grissets and cressets, and fuddling cups and frizzens, crocks and pounce-boxes, trivets and spiders, druggets and gorgets, swifts and quirts, scows and scrubraces, flip-irons and gallipots. What could 'foofarraw' possibly mean? Nothing less than all the finery that mountain men, borrowing from their fellow French trappers' *fanfaron*, like to deck out their wives in—bright-coloured clothes, sleigh-bells, bangles, looking-glasses and anything else that might make one shine more brightly than the others, including in one case, 'a broad, glazed leather St Louis fireman's belt . . . marked "Central" in large gold letters!' Would you recognise an iron apple-peeler if you saw one, or an eeling fork, come to that, or a bootjack shaped like some strange hybrid creature? Or an amusette?—which has nothing to do with *soubrettes* but something to do with playthings like firearms. Top marks if you know that a 'bouge' is the curved part of a plate connecting rim and bottom. You might know who Mary Jane is, but do you know what a 'Mary Ann' is? And amid the proliferation of synthetic fabrics, don't you long for homespun and linsey-wolsey, dimity, chintz, lawn, and batiste? And when you think about it, what does resist printing resist and discharge printing discharge? Why, dye, of course, the sort of thing you would dearly love to know about when the purple in your favourite

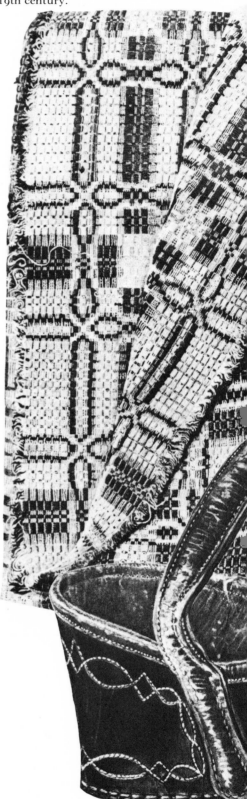

32. Reversible blue and white woven blanket made in New Jersey early in the 19th century. This is a more intricate type of weaving than the easiest of all types, the overshot weave done on the four-harness loom found in almost every home from Colonial times through the 19th century.

33. Black leather basket lined with red made by slaves on a plantation in Virginia in the 19th century. There seems little doubt that negro artisans played a vital role in the progress of plantation manufactures in the South.

Indian cotton blouse starts tie-dying the white! How's your Pennsylvania German on *schmalz schmelzer* (fat melter) and your Spanish perceptions in lariat (*la reata*) and lasso (*el lazo*)? Before the game is over, you will be mesmerised by names and objects and find yourself going around in wide-eyed wonder.

But whilst it is fun and often informative and illuminating to linger and puzzle over all these things, as books like the recent *Wisconsin Death Trip* show, it is sheer wishful thinking to believe, as many people do, today, that country-living more than a hundred years ago was happier and less troubled than our own uneasy, primarily urban times. Financial machination and contagious disease were commonplace, so was suicide, arson and insanity. The American Dream of fecundity and expansionism, of pioneering adventure and the fertility of the earth, often gave way to a nightmarish reality in rural America, which should give pause to those who hanker not just for the things of the past, but the whole way of life.

Many a commune has gone back to the land and the old hard ways of doing things; a self-conscious, sometimes pretentious return to laborious ways of earning a living, or simply of living as one young lady corrected me rather primly recently. She was giving a demonstration of how yarn was dyed, carded and spun a hundred years ago, but, alas, in my opinion, her colours were dull and the yarn very coarse. What is old and antique is not by definition better than what is new.

One well known collector of Walpoleana says it does not really matter *what* you collect, as long as you collect it passionately, whether it is nails or sardine-tin keys, music-rolls or hearing-aids, luggage-tags or rings, fluting-irons or spectacles, nickels made of wood, fire-extinguishers made of glass, or bookends with a hood. And yet . . . and yet. . . . At some point in the collecting game comparisons start creeping in, especially if you are not merely a magpie. You may want to know if your treasures were made better in one place than in another, and perhaps best of all at a certain time. Every speciality has its inside rules. For the purist collector of dime novels (sensational adventure stories which are thought to have made their first appearance about 1860), many stories once sold for the 10¢ or dime of the title do not qualify for the collector's attention because they are love stories, English or American classics, or translations from the French. Only blood and thunder originals, in which the heroines are meant to be rescued not kissed, do, and some of these stories sold for a nickel or 5¢.

The earliest kind of criteria set such standards as originality of design, fine hand-tooling and unconventional colour patterns. But what criteria should be used to assess the products of mass-production? Is there such a thing as

34. Today's feminists would be up in arms against Harriet
Sublett who, with a little editing from me, worked the following
lines into her sampler early in the 19th century:
Naked in nothing shall a woman be.
But veil her very wit with modesty,
Let man discover. Let not her display,
But yield her charms of mind with sweet delay.

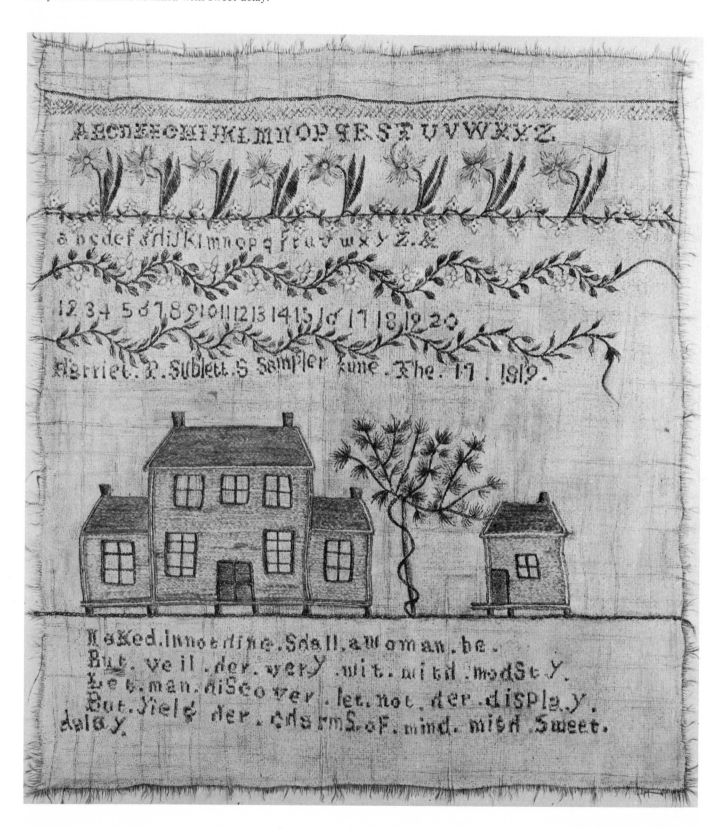

35. A linen sampler embroidered with silks.

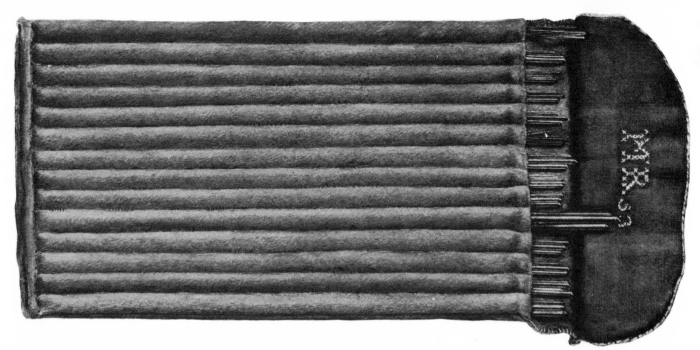

industrial art? The London *Times* rashly scoffed at the
grotesque appearance of Cyrus McCormick's reaper when it
was exhibited in London at the Great Exhibition of 1851. But
The Times soon had to revise its opinions when the machine
proved its superiority in the field. If you have an insatiable
visual appetite, a keen eye for detail as well as for artistic
quality, a sense of history, and boundless energy, you will
delight in 'junking around', in sorting out the fakes, the
miserable restorations, the mistaken and vainglorious
attributions and the poor taste, and you will try to avoid, or
indulge in the fads and fashions of collecting, because that is
all part of the game. One doleful householder told me recently,
pointing to a crateful of glass insulators from telegraph wires,
'We were sellin' 'em like hotcakes only a few years ago, but
nobody seems to want 'em anymore.' Only if you are lucky
will you discover that the French General Rochambeau
camped in your backyard on his way to the Battle of Yorktown
at the end of the War of Independence in 1781, and left
behind coins and soldiers' buttons aplenty and underneath
those maybe even a few paleo-Indian projectile points! There
is plenty of leg-work and brain-work still to be done.

What we do know is that wood was the first material
readily available to the first settlers. It was all over the place
and consequently cheap well into the 19th century. Wooden
utensils are usually called 'treenware'—made from trees. White
oak was popular for casks because of its hardness and strength.
Other hard woods, such as maple and walnut, were used for
butter moulds, which had to withstand continual scalding.
Mortars, bowls and spoons were made from the burls or
knots of those woods, while fruitwoods were used for tea
caddies with hinged tops and locks and shaped like apples and
pears.

36. The Shakers believed that there was
a place for everything and that everything should be in its place as is clear
from this knitting needle case made of
broadcloth and lined with flannel
perhaps by a Shaker crafts*woman* in the
19th century. In one of the more
colourful descriptions of the wagon-
trains taking settlers into the west we
are asked to listen for the click of
knitting needles in steady counterpoint
to the creeking of wagon wheels and the
jingle of harness.

37. Tin candle mould filler thought to
have been made in Virginia, probably
late in the 18th or early in the 19th
century. Itinerant candlemakers were
among the numerous hawkers and
walkers roaming the countryside in
search of business in the 19th century.

38. Early 19th-century flat-iron holder
made of wrought iron.

Some of the most attractive treenware was made by the Pennsylvania Germans, who decorated objects such as butter moulds with cows, eagles, tulips and hearts, and a design resembling the hex sign seen on the sides of their barns, and variously interpreted as a way of warding off evil, or just as pure decoration. Examples of the work of one identified craftsman, Joseph Lehn—egg-cups, open salts, saffron boxes and a penny bank—can be seen in the Pennsylvania Farm Museum in Landis Valley, Lancaster, Pennsylvania.

Wooden flails, shovels, and piggins or scoops, were standard in the rice-growing fields of the Carolinas after the crop was introduced there towards the end of the 17th century.

Baskets, used for collecting eggs, gathering wild berries from the woods, and fruit and vegetables from the garden or the local market, were probably the most common containers in rural America. Willow reeds or oziers were most frequently used because they were pliable and strong, and the forms were mostly simple.

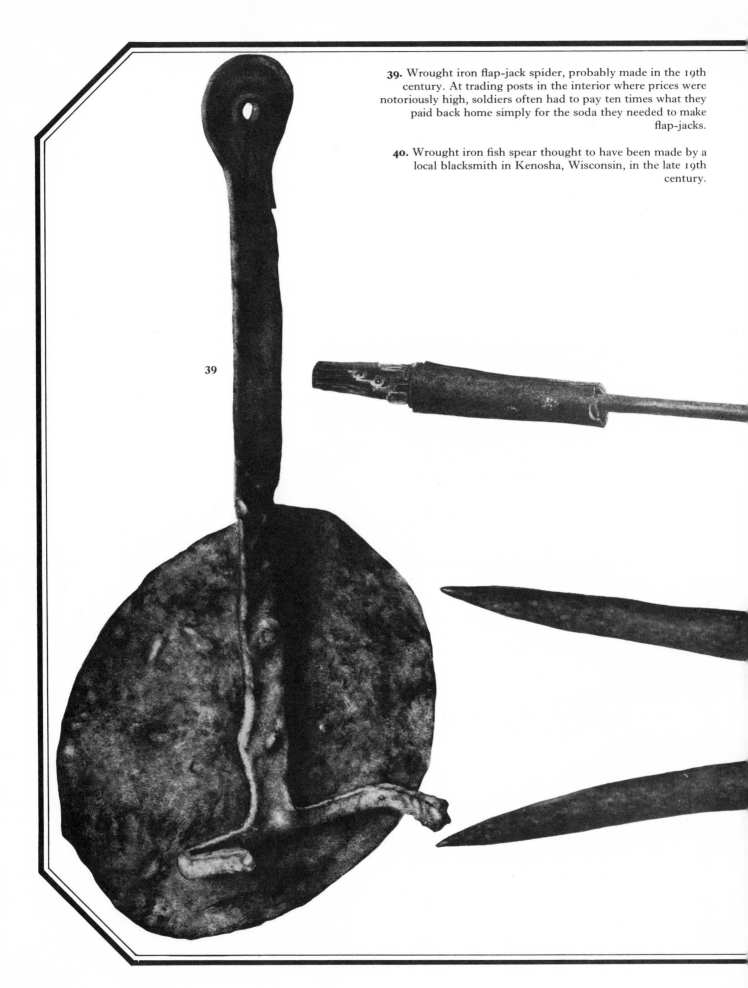

39. Wrought iron flap-jack spider, probably made in the 19th century. At trading posts in the interior where prices were notoriously high, soldiers often had to pay ten times what they paid back home simply for the soda they needed to make flap-jacks.

40. Wrought iron fish spear thought to have been made by a local blacksmith in Kenosha, Wisconsin, in the late 19th century.

39

41. Wrought iron digging tool approximately two-thirds actual size made about 1810 probably by Indian neophytes under the direction of a Spanish American priest/ironsmith or soldier/ironsmith at the San Buenaventura Mission, Ventura, California.

42. A kilogramme scale probably made back East about 1840 but used in Wisconsin where it now lives in the care of the Milwaukee Historical Society. The hooks, links and pointer are iron and a brass plate showing the weights is fitted inside a steel band.

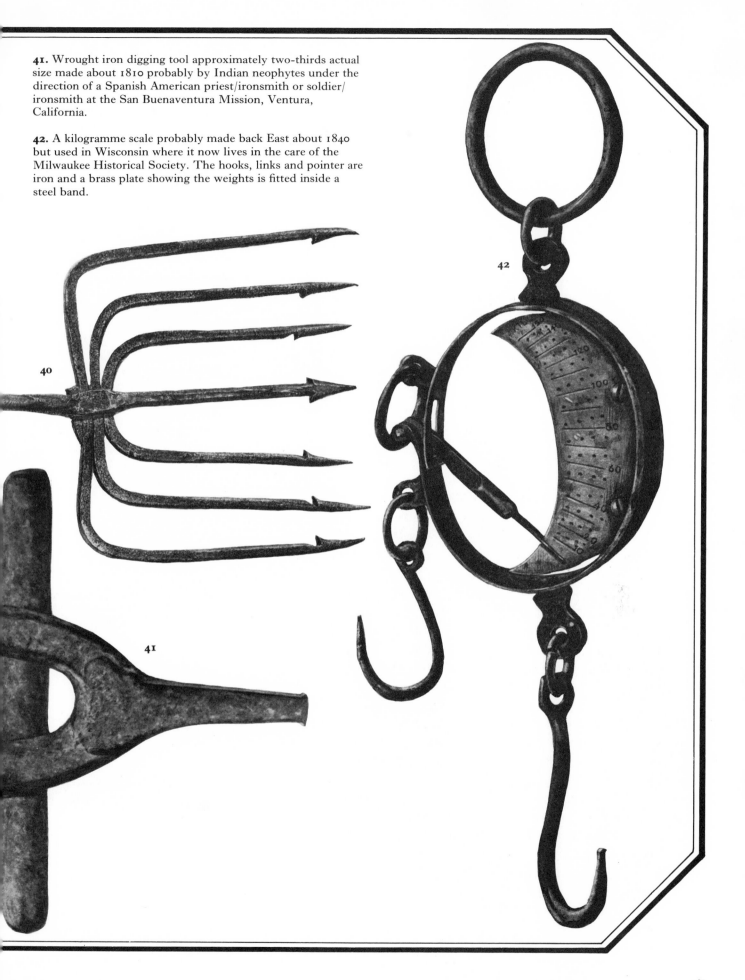

Then there was iron. Blacksmiths headed the list of tradesmen solicited by the Virginia Company for the settlement at Jamestown in 1608, but the beginnings of a new industry there were not promising. By the late 18th century, however, the American Colonies were producing more iron than England was, in part because of the vast reserves of wood. Iron bars were shipped to England in considerable quantities from New England, Virginia and Pennsylvania, and often returned in the form of finished goods.

No one has yet devised a foolproof method of distinguishing the locally made from the imported. But the characteristics that have come to be regarded as typically American are simplicity, lack of ostentatious ornament, and, as always, the appearance of utility. The whorls and scrolls and other purely decorative effects in Old World iron are conspicuously absent. Even the Pennsylvania German work, probably the most intricate of any done here, shows a certain restraint and simplicity. Whether this was because over-elaborate ornament was distasteful to the residents of a country with the frontier on its doorstep, or because the Colonial spirit rebelled against anything that smacked of ostentation, is still debatable. The plain appearance of most Colonial ironwork may simply have resulted from such practical considerations as the high price of a blacksmith's labour, or the limited resources and skill of individual smiths.

Cast iron, shaped by being poured into moulds while still in a molten state, as opposed to wrought iron, which is worked and welded in a forge, has been made here since the first furnace was lit at Jamestown. Much of the ornamental ironwork of the South—the railings and grillwork of Charleston and New Orleans, for example—was cast. So wrought iron snobs beware!

Steel was extremely rare in America before the Civil War, its use confined to cutting tools. Some axes, for example, have steel cutting edges forge-welded on to them. Steel production began in earnest after the Civil War.

By the mid 19th century over sixty different ploughs 'generally made of cast iron' had been shaped for a specific purpose: 'rootbreakers, prairie, meadow, stubble, selfsharpener, corn, cotton, rice, sugar cane, subsoil and hillside land' as stated in the 1848 catalogue of the New York manufacturer, A. and B. Allen & Co.

In the kitchen and around the fireside there were andirons and trivets, toasters, spits, hooks and trammels, countless varieties of ladles, skimmers, spoons, forks, some with contrasting metals, such as brass or copper, cleverly inlaid in the handles. Since many of these pieces were made to order, you might, if you are lucky, find a signed and/or dated piece in this group.

Regional characteristics have been noted in hinges,

43. Cast iron bootjack of the late 19th century. But what kind of creature is that with the body of an insect and the feet of a turtle?

hasps, shutter fasteners, and foot scrapers; and nails are becoming a specialised study all to themselves. The stories that the early settlers burnt down their homes when they left them in order to pick up the nails, seem questionable. Basic research still has to be done on the origin of the often exquisitely fashioned hinges and catches and other cabinet-making hardware for chests, boxes and furniture.

Heating stoves were cast as early as 1728, and were particularly popular with German immigrants. The English settlers appear to have stuck to their open fireplaces for longer. The plates used around the furnaces were cast in various patterns including some biblical and stylised ones. They were sometimes named after women in the family, hence the four known Mary Ann furnaces of 18th-century Pennsylvania. The Franklin stove—the original was invented by Benjamin—is an open hearth type decorated with a variety of motifs, as fashion dictated. Collectors of advertising tokens recently dusted off their treasures to show a world, threatened by a shortage of homeheating oil, what a coalburning 'German Heater' made in Illinois in the 1870s looked like.

The Jamestown crowd also tried their hands at pottery, but, as in many another trade, nothing got really started in this one until the latter part of the 18th century. Earthenware or 'erthingwear', as it sometimes appeared rather charmingly in early advertisements—literally anything made of earth, or at least clay—should strictly speaking refer to all pots made of such. But there are clays and clays, and the discerning would shudder to hear porcelain called 'earthenware' and the arty would do likewise if their ceramics were so labelled. Earthenware is countryware, a little coarse, maybe, but, as in the redware and stoneware made in America mainly in the 19th century, not without its charms.

The clay needed for redware and for red bricks and roof tiles was to be found, like the fuel needed to heat the kilns, all over the place. It has traces of iron oxide in it, and they are the cause of the various shades of red produced in the firing process. And not much was needed in the way of equipment apart from a horse-powered mill for grinding and mixing the clays and a home-made potter's wheel and kiln. Result—cheaper wares than those imported from England. Country people, moreover, were a bit out of reach of the agents supplying English goods, so that among the numerous redware articles are such essentials as dishes and bowls, cups and mugs, basins, jelly and cake moulds, herb pots, crocks, milk-pans, churns and flower-pots, not to mention spill holders and bird whistles, kegs and water-carriers.

Various kinds of decoration are found on redware, some planned, some unplanned. Unsuspected impurities in the clay, or unusually high temperatures in the kiln, could produce

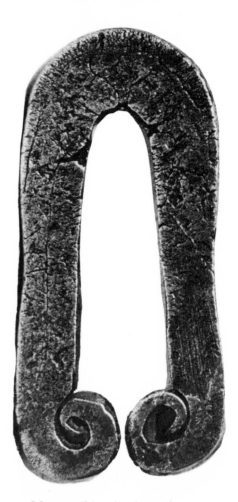

44. Mystery object for those of us brought up with safety matches. This is a fire steel thought to have been made by a pioneer settler in northern California about 1850. With a flint to strike against the steel and tinder to catch the first spark, you had fire. Charles Dickens once complained that it took half an hour to light a fire with flint and steel.

45. A rare early 19th-century carpet known as the Caswell carpet after the original owner in Vermont. Each of the small rectangular panels that make up the carpet was embroidered on a tambour frame in double Kensington stitch, a chain stitch made with a crochet hook through a coarse foundation fabric. The long panel at left fitted over the hearth in seasons when there was no fire.

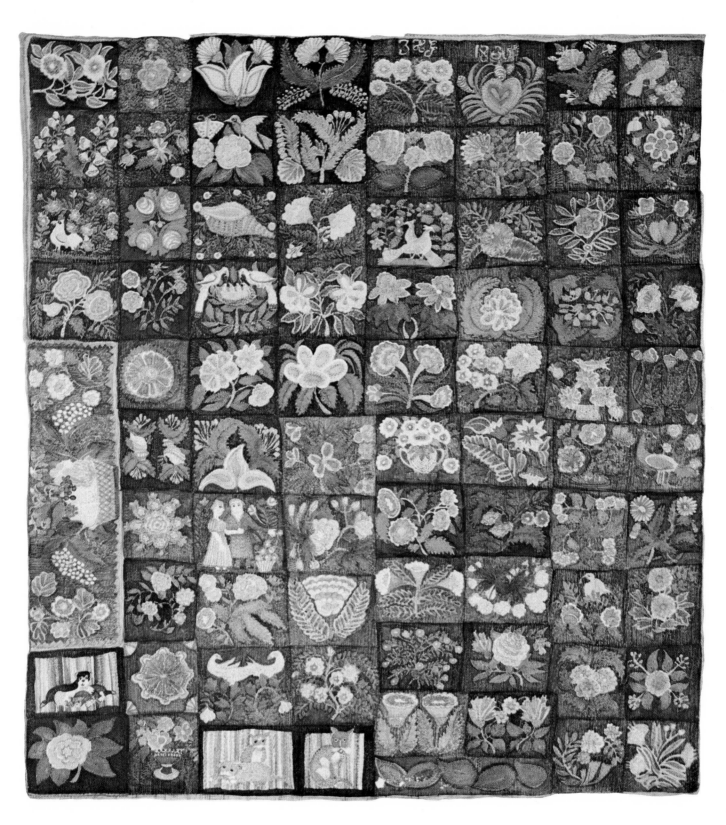

some surprisingly interesting, decorative streaks or mottling in brown, green, orange and red, for example. A planned change in the colours was also achieved by adding oxides to the glaze: copper for green—used sparingly because it was expensive— and inexpensive manganese for yellows, browns and blacks. The basic red was retained by using a pure form of lead glaze, which is transparent with a yellowish tinge. Simple designs such as scrolls, dots, names and mottoes, or pleas of one sort or another, were applied with cream-coloured slip or liquid clay. The Pennsylvania potters, however, were much more ambitious with their slip decoration. They immersed a piece in a thin coating of slip and then scratched out various, often intricate, designs, letting the redware show through, an ancient technique commonly known as *sgraffito*, meaning 'scratched'.

Potters went west with a lot of other people and put down roots in Ohio in particular, where a blending of New England and Pennsylvania traditions has been noted. One group, the Society of Separatists or Zoarites, gave their name— Zoarware—to a type of redware which was usually glazed

46. Bronze and brass scales for weighing gold—a key precision instrument needed in the delicate process of assaying the rich finds of the Gold Rush days in the latter part of the 19th century. These scales were made in San Francisco but were found in Nevada. An estimated 20,000 men are said to have rushed to Washoe, Nevada, after the news leaked out about the Comstock lode—a rich vein of gold and silver discovered by Henry Comstock and a few friends in 1859.

yellow or buff-coloured. Systematic studies still remain to be done in identifying the output of numerous other potteries that by the second half of the 19th century had opened up in the Mid-West in places like Illinois, Iowa, Minnesota and Nebraska Territory.

There are some redware fakes. The darkening of the glaze as a result of acids in food or of cooking heat, and any kind of scratching, from knives or anything else, can be and has been imitated, for example.

Stoneware, mostly a whiteish, greyish colour, is made from finer, denser clays than redware, and they were not so widely available. In fact, the best type was found only in New Jersey, the New York area, and Ohio. Fine grades of stoneware are said to approach the quality of porcelain. By the end of the 19th century, the American output of stoneware – crocks for pickles and butter, jams and preserves, and jugs for home-made wines or vinegar or pancake batter, and the like – was estimated at more than four times that of redware.

One reason for the emergence of stoneware seems to have been the pother everyone was in over the lead glaze used on redware, and its possible poisonous effects. The *Pennsylvania Mercury* stated the case rather luridly on 4 February 1785, saying that the lead glaze, attacked by acid foods, 'becomes a slow but sure poison, chiefly affecting the Nerves, that enfeebles the constitution, and produces paleness, tremours, gripes, palsies, etc.' Most people seem to have felt that the better part of wisdom was to switch to stoneware for which 'no other glazing need be used than what is produced by a little common salt strewed over the ware'. This produced a roughish, colourless, glassy coating.

The most common kind of decoration on stoneware is freehand painting or stencils, usually in blue (because cobalt was one of the few substances that could withstand the high temperatures required to fire stoneware), of birds and flowers, real and imaginary, and decorative details, such as scrolls, names, dates and initials. One Ohioan maker, E. B. Hall, is thought to have originated a clasped hands design. He is also said to have worked best big – four gallons and up.

The Bell family of potters, working in the Shenandoah Valley in Maryland, and Virginia, made notable redware and stoneware. Some experts consider that their distinctive flowing designs of birds, for example, are Oriental in feeling.

Potters were pedlars, too, and bartered their stock around the countryside for tobacco, meat, corn, and tar which was needed for a variety of purposes. Some were minutemen. No less than twenty-two potters from the small town of Peabody, Massachusetts, answered the call to the Battle for Independence at Lexington in 1775.

Pottery is less perishable than some other kinds of antiques, and the collector lucky enough to come across a piece carefully wrapped up and put away for a rainy day or a special occasion and never brought out, will find it as fresh as the day it left the potter's hands.

Somewhere betwixt and between the whipped cream and the bread and butter is pewter, an alloy of 80–90 per cent tin and the rest copper. Copper was locally available but the main ingredient, tin, had to be imported from you-know-who. The duty on tin bars made it impossible for local pewterers to compete with the finished English products, which came in duty free, so they mostly had to content themselves with reworking and recasting old or spoilt pieces (which had perhaps been left too close to an open hearth), and fill in their time as farmers, blacksmiths, tavernkeepers, or merchants of one sort or another. Not many of them bothered to sign their work, although unmarked pewter is not always American-made. Those who did mark their wares—plates, porringers or small soup bowls, beakers, spoons and so on—worked in the more affluent East coast cities. And many of them may not have had the right to use a mark under the strict rules governing the members of London's Worshipful Company of Pewterers. The

47. Branding iron. In the decade after the Civil War, the Great Plains west of the Mississippi were transformed into a gigantic reservoir of cattle, herds spreading out over the open range across a dozen States from Texas to Montana Territory (which became a State in 1889). To reduce the chance of loss— accidental or otherwise—each rancher had his own brand registered in an official Brand Book. A favourite sport of cattle thieves or '"rustlers" as the lawless desperadoes who abound in Arizona, New Mexico and Texas are called' was altering brands. This was usually accomplished with a straight iron rod slightly curved at the marking/ altering end to facilitate the change of a T to a curry comb with three or more teeth, to add flying curves and rockers to a W or to put a box around any mark.

48. The Stemple and Lincoln coach at the Gould Stage. This photograph dates from about 1870. John Judkyn Memorial, Bath.

49. 19th-century hooked rug using a variation of the Star of Bethlehem design commonly found on patchwork quilts.

50. Syntax, spelling and punctuation sometimes go awry in the not always easily decipherable pleas or moral exhortations found on early 19th-century samplers such as this. But this is carping when the overall achievement is so charming.

51. Hammered copper cruet made around the turn of the 18th century in a Spanish Californian Mission, probably by Indian neophytes under the direction of a priest or lay craftsman.

52. Punched tin coffee pot made about 1835 by J. Shade, a Pennsylvania craftsman whose name appears on the handle. The same design of peacocks, crest and foliage is on both sides.

53. Sheet tin candleholder with a natural finish made in the late 18th century by an unknown craftsman in what is now New Mexico.

craftsman had more freedom—not to say licence—on these shores. Limited in materials and moulds, as far as pewter was concerned, they used their freedom to attain clean, unpretentious lines. The ambition to decorate was lavished only on the handles of porringers, which often followed the English style of pierced open work. Applicable or not, we can, consequently, all begin to understand the doggerel that says,

> When every blessed thing you hold
> Is made of silver, or of gold,
> You long for simple pewter.

Sheet tin or tin-plate (sheets of thinly rolled iron coated with tin), had distinct advantages over iron for the housewife, in that it made lighter pots and pails and was easier to clean. It was also cheaper than pewter or brass, for example. Pressing local demand meant that local tinsmiths were kept busy, even though they were dependent on that tiresome Old Country for their supplies of the new material. (A rolling mill for producing thin, smooth sheets of iron had been invented in Britain towards the end of the 17th century. And since Britain, in addition, had a virtual monopoly on tin resources at the time, the country had no trouble at all in controlling the tin-plate market for years to come.)

Two Irish immigrants, Edward and William Pattison, are credited with setting up the American tinware industry when they put down roots in what is now Berlin, Connecticut, about 1740. Connecticut remained the centre of the industry well into the 19th century. Edward Pattison is also credited with inaugurating what turned out to be a very effective system of marketing, when he hired pedlars to hawk his products in neighbouring towns. As roads were opened up, Connecticut wares were taken north to Canada and into the South and Mid-West of the United States.

A wide and wonderful variety of plain tinware is listed in trade catalogues and advertisements, from candle boxes and candle moulds, to gingerbread cutters and graters, skimmers and strainers, 'moulds for blomonges', coffee 'biggins'—a type of coffee-pot invented by a gentleman of that name, which contained a strainer that prevented the coffee grounds mixing with the infusion—speaking and hearing trumpets, foot stoves for travellers, 'bathing machines', or 'salvatories'.

In the West, tin cups and coffee-pots are often mentioned in camp fire stories. One such story tells of two friends, who, when they had nothing better to do, filled tin cups with whisky and took turns at shooting them off the top of each other's heads. One winter the two friends fell out in a fit of what came to be called 'cabin fever', with the inevitable result that when they played their dangerous game, the first shot went not through a tin cup, but through a human head.

Decorated tinware, sometimes called japanned or

54. Painted tin coffee pot probably made in Pennsylvania around the turn of the 18th century.

55. Pennsylvania German earthenware gravy-boat or water whistle. You blow through the head if you want to whistle, after you have filled the body with water, of course. The neck length apparently governs the pitch!

56. Painted tin box used for valuable papers or jewels or money probably made in Maine early in the 19th century. The maker probably learned his trade in Berlin, Connecticut, where the tin industry was established as early as 1740. The scratched initials on the box suggest it may have been made by Oliver Buckley for his daughter. Buckley is known to have worked as a tinsmith in Berlin, Connecticut, before moving to Maine. He is said to have had a liking for circles—among other things—in his decorative work.

59

tôleware (the French call it *tôle peinte*), has survived in larger
quantities, perhaps because it was less used and better cared
for, or perhaps because the paint and varnish with which it was
decorated gave a certain amount of protection against wear
and tear. Britain also exported large quantities of decorated
tinware to America, but a distinctive local style has been noted
in pieces from Berlin, Connecticut, which influenced work in
nearby Maine, as well as New York and Pennsylvania. Some of
the decoration was done freehand, but the most easily
recognised Berlin work was done from stencils. Women and
girls seem to have been responsible for most of the American
japanning of tinware.

A quite different type of decorative tinwork was done in
what is now New Mexico, particularly after the area became
part of the United States in 1846, and tin boxes, candle moulds
and mirror frames, and supplies of one sort or another, were
taken along the Santa Fe Trail into the area in tin containers.
The local smiths cut up whatever discarded tin they could put
their hands on and reworked it into fanciful frames, *nichos*
(small shrines), candlesconces, processional staves and crosses,
often patiently soldered together from many tiny scraps, some
of which retained a lard brand or other commercial trademark,
or even directions for opening a tin can! Surface decoration,
strongly influenced by leatherwork, was punched with nails,
cold chisels and small dies in small, often repeated geometric
patterns. Rosettes of graduated, scalloped tin discs were wired
to the main piece, or as with flying scrolls, for example,
soldered to it. They were never painted. The colouring found
on some pieces was probably a later addition.

Glass bottles and fancier glassware are also known to
have added a splash of colour and shapeliness to many a
country home, but as mentioned earlier, have become the
subject of specialised study, and consequently get only a
passing mention here.

Textiles, too, have become the subject of specialised
study, and inspiration for many a Pop Artist and 'folk optic'
fabric of our own day, but since quilts have become for me
a sort of emblem for this book, and since, after all, the
original American flag was a patchwork, they deserve a little
more attention here, particularly the quilt-makers.

In what is called the 'Hat and Fragrance Unit' at the
Shelburne Museum in Vermont, where one of the country's
outstanding textile collections is housed in what used to be the
Shelburne Town Hall barn, you can linger over many of the
quilts and coverlets in the collection, almost as easily as you
would the pages of a book, because they are mounted for easy
viewing on hinged moveable racks.

What a joy in geometry is there! What variations on
simple box and diamond motifs! What charm in the free-style
appliqués! Here the crafts*woman* comes into her own, and since

57. Pewter charger—the big one—of the early 18th century and pewter plate of the early 19th century. Plates—a smooth rim type as here and a single reeded type—are among the most numerous of the known surviving American-made pewter objects. The brass ladle is a rare marked American example also of the early 19th century.

58. Gray stoneware crock made at Corlears Hook, New York.

59. Gray stoneware jar with blue lettering and decoration made in 1799 by Clarkson Crolius Sr. of New York, a grandson of the founder of a dynasty of some 15 potters, William 'Crolyas', who started 'the first stoneware kiln or furnace . . . in this year 1730' on Potbaker's Hill, on lower Manhattan Island.

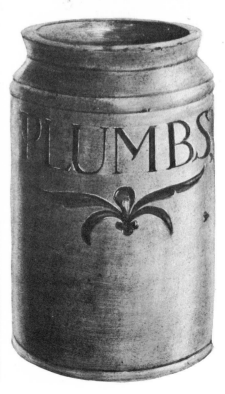

60. Pennsylvania German illuminated birth certificate.

61. Detail from the rare Caswell carpet now in New York's Metropolitan Museum—a courting couple, perhaps, or newly-weds, Mr & Mrs Caswell themselves, or maybe Adam and Eve.

62. Saddle blanket made by an Indian woman living near the San Antonio Mission, Jolon, California in the late 19th century. An apishamore—just in case you didn't know—is a saddle blanket made out of the robe or skin of a buffalo calf, and/or a bed, presumably of the same material. Strouding, on the other hand, according to one definition, was 'a kind of cheap cloth . . . made from woollen rags . . . exported to the North American Indians'.

she could not afford the luxury of more classical forms of needlework, proceeded, if not to invent, at least to develop to a high degree a method of working with cloth considered America's own – patchwork quilting, a way of using up otherwise useless pieces of material at a time when textiles were extremely valuable.

There are essentially two types of patchwork designs, those that are pieced together and those that are applied or *appliquéd*, but their names are legion and do not always bear a self-evident relationship to the design. Moreover, as mentioned earlier, the same pattern can have more than one name. A Bear's-Paw in Ohio is a Duck's-Foot-in-the-Mud on Long Island and a Hand-of-Friendship in Philadelphia. Other names like London Road, Ocean Waves, Road to California, Kansas Troubles, Wagon Tracks, Fanny's Fan, Birds-in-the-Window, show how much history, domestic and political, was worked into these artistic productions.

The quilting, too – a utilitarian necessity needed to keep the filling or lining in place when the decorative top was stitched to the plain or also decorated bottom or backing – has fanciful names galore, from the more complicated designs worked from templates such as Princess Feather, Peacock Fan and Spider's Web, to the simpler freehand crossbars and diamonds. *Trapunto*, or Italian quilting, is the name given to stuffed designs formed by the quilting alone. One such quilt, which is considered an extraordinary example of stitchery around a pineapple design, is thought to have been the work of slaves on a Missouri plantation about the middle of the 19th century.

It became the custom in 19th-century America for an unmarried girl to make thirteen patchwork quilts as part of her dowry. When the announcement of her betrothal was made, all her neighbours and friends would gather together to help 'quilt her tops', the final stage in the quilt-making process saved for just such an announcement. It must have taken several quilting bees to put together all thirteen quilts! The thirteenth quilt, not usually made until after the betrothal was announced, might take the form of a friendship or album quilt for which friends and relatives made sections which were pieced together at the party! Not all the parties or quilting bees were prompted by weddings in the offing, of course.

Much more rare than the quilts – only forty examples are known – are a group of embroidered bed rugs dating mainly from the 18th century, whose entire surface is covered with running or darning stitches made with from one to sixteen strands of wool, sometimes cut to give a luxurious pile. Most of them are dated and initialled and were probably prized as family heirlooms. Thirty-four of them were brought together in what is believed to be the first exhibition of its kind, at the Wadsworth Atheneum in Hartford, Connecticut in 1972.

63. Toy oxcart and figures carved by a Vermont farmer and his son in about 1860. Essex Institute, Salem, Massachusetts.

64. 'Dr Busby', a favourite American card game of the 19th century.

65. Daintily dressed rag doll with a painted face and hair probably made in Pennsylvania about 1860. These soft cuddly creatures were very popular.

ALONG THE TRAIL

'No people in the world are such great travellers as the Americans' wrote a correspondent for London's *Penny Magazine* in 1838. 'I have no doubt that the newness of the country is the primary and chief cause of the erratic disposition of the Americans;' he went on, '. . . unlike the inhabitants of older and thickly settled communities, the great bulk of the rural population is composed of sojourners and wanderers. The farmers or more properly the pioneers of the country are not more erratic than the commercial and trading portion of the community; for a storekeeper in a small country village or at some "four-corners" (cross roads) will not only travel twice in the year to some seaport two or three hundred miles off, but he will go as far in some other direction to lay in a stock of cast-iron or earthenware, "notions" as the country may produce, besides during the proper season he will probably scour the country in search of such cattle as it may seem advisable for him to drive to the distant market.'

By the middle of the 18th century pedlars and stage coaches had been making their way with increasing frequency along the network of roads crisscrossing the interior of New England and connecting Philadelphia, the largest Colonial city, with the rest of Pennsylvania and New Jersey. In the South, the westward migration was made easier when a Virginia physician and surveyor, Dr Thomas Walker, discovered the

66. Red sandstone towering in the background, the scene is the Canyon de Chelly on the Navajo Indian Reservation in Arizona. The year is 1903 and this unhappy traveller is contemplating his broken wagon, the pieces of which, we are told, have all been saved.

No. 94---Supply

R. Views ross the Continent, West from Omaha. ⟶s, Last Siding, C. Peck's Outfit.

Cumberland Gap, a natural passage through the mountains separating Virginia from what became Kentucky and Tennessee. Courageous and determined men like Daniel Boone—hunter, marksman, scout, guide—made it into the Wilderness Trail, one of the most important pioneer routes west.

But beyond the Cumberland Gap there was a more threatening barrier to westward expansion in the late 18th century—the French, who had set up a long line of forts from Canada south into the Mississippi Valley in an attempt to confine the English colonies east of the Appalachian Mountains. It cost the British and the colonists dear to stop them, but stop them they did, and at the end of the War of Independence in 1783, the new Republic's western frontier was the Mississippi. In 1803, President Thomas Jefferson purchased from the Emperor Napoleon for the paltry sum of $16 million, or an estimated 4¢ an acre, the huge central area of the country west of the Mississippi to the Rocky Mountains, known as the Louisiana Purchase. This brought the new republic's holdings up against those of the Spanish Empire, in the south west, not to mention those of the Russian and the British again in the north west. After more warring and haggling, by 1850, the new western frontier was the Pacific Ocean. We will perhaps never know what Lewis and Clark's first impression of the Pacific Ocean was—if they ever recorded it. The entry in the diary they kept of their assignment from President Jefferson to explore and map the lands of the Louisiana Purchase, appears to be missing for the day of their arrival on the Oregon coast in November 1805.

The lure of the West has for centuries been the hope of the great wealth to be found there. As early as 1536, word reached Mexico City of fabulous cities with streets paved in gold and walls studded with precious jewels somewhere in the vast deserts to the north. In 1540 Francisco Vasquez de Coronado led an expedition in search of the Seven Cities of Cibola, as the mythical cities had come to be known, and discovered they were 'seven little villages'. More than four centuries were to pass before gold and silver were discovered in California and Colorado. But in the interval there were other riches ripe for exploitation in the West.

First there was the fur trade, particularly in beaver skins, the material from which the finest hats had been made in Europe for more than four centuries, only to be displaced in the 1830s by silk. Brass tags used for identifying bundles of furs shipped down the Missouri are a humble reminder of the trade in which John Jacob Astor, for example, made his fortune. More still has to be learned about the Rocky Mountain rendez-vous, the annual trade fairs of the 1820s and 1830s, when trappers and traders gathered in a pre-arranged spot to exchange pelts for vital supplies. Interestingly enough, the word 'dicker' used since ancient times in reckoning skins or hides, was early extended in American usage to mean all trade by barter.

In the south west the abundance of buck skins and buffalo hides meant that trunks and ore and water buckets, winnowing sieves and door-pulls, grain sacks, saddle bags, even panels for church paintings, as well as coats and shields, breeches and shirts, were made of leather. (Leather clothing was quite common in the East, too, which, as one expert has pointed out, was sometimes called 'the land of the bucksin breeches').

Then there were the timber booms starting in the 1820s as Europe's supplies were being exhausted. Lumbermen by the thousands swarmed into Wisconsin, Michigan and northern Illinois, until the region was stripped of its tall white pine. The portentous like to talk of a great nation being built where once only a great forest stood. The lumbermen have a better way of putting it. According to one of their stories, their legendary hero, Paul Bunyan, could cut the pine off forty acres with a single swing of his axe, while his ox, Babe, could reverse the current of the Mississippi with a single draught!

There was good, cheap farm land, too, once the forests were cleared, or out on the prairie. At a meeting of the Western History Association at Yale University in 1972, one of the speakers said, 'We have to deromanticise the West somewhat, to play up the farmboy and downplay the cowboy' and went on to make a passionate attack on the gun culture born of frontier violence. Some historians are now concerned, however, that new myths will replace the old. 'The new recognition being given to the role of Indians, blacks and Chicanos is greatly expanding our perspective on Western history' the association's president said, 'but it won't help our perspective if this interest takes on the qualities of a moral crusade'. When Francis Parkman, author of *The Oregon Trail*, took his tour of curiosity and amusement to the Rocky Mountains, he noted some of the motives for going west: the insane hope of a better condition of life, the desire to shake off all restraints of law and society, restlessness. But he also noted, 'The sons of civilization, drawn by the fascinations of a fresher and bolder life, thronged to the western wilds in multitudes which blighted the charm that lured them' and considered it 'certain that multitudes bitterly repent the journey, and after they reach the land of promise are happy enough to escape it.'

In 1813, the Missouri Gazette had made the momentous announcement, 'It appears that a journey across the continent of North America might be performed with a waggon, there being no obstruction in the whole route that any person would dare to call a mountain'. The paper was

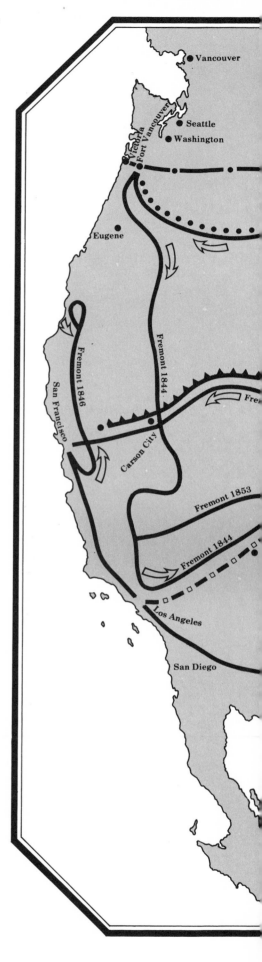

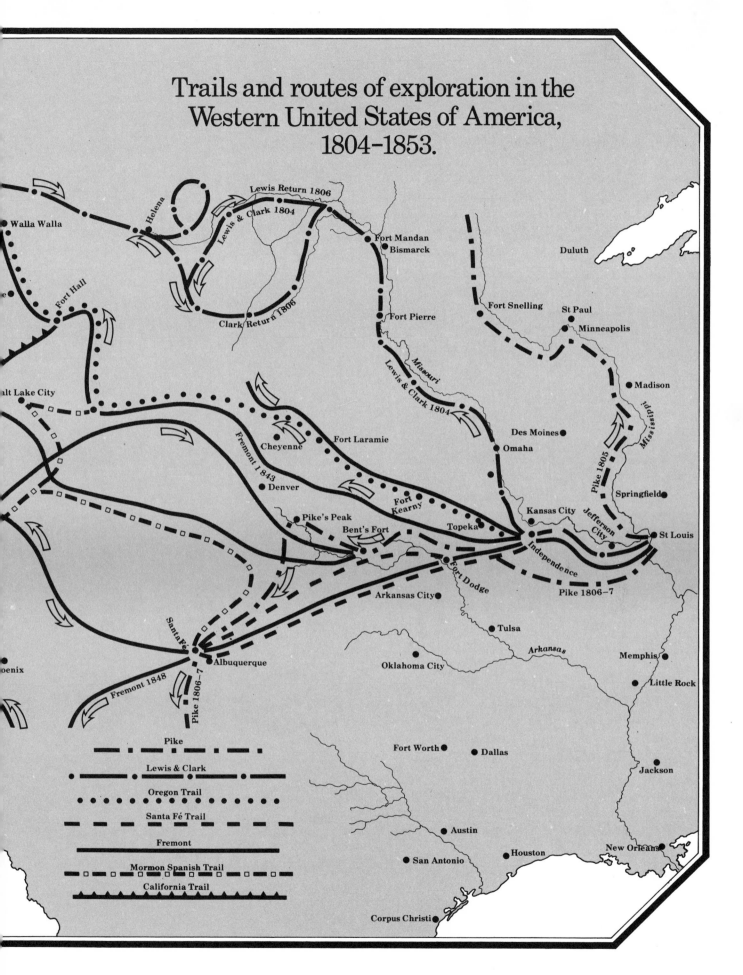

Trails and routes of exploration in the Western United States of America, 1804–1853.

Walla Walla
Helena
Fort Hall
Lewis Return 1806
Lewis & Clark 1804
Clark Return 1806
Fort Mandan
Bismarck
Duluth
Fort Snelling
St Paul
Minneapolis
Fort Pierre
alt Lake City
Missouri
Lewis & Clark 1804
Des Moines
Omaha
Madison
Mississippi
Fremont 1843
Cheyenne
Fort Laramie
Denver
Pike's Peak
Fort Kearny
Bent's Fort
Topeka
Kansas City
Jefferson City
Pike 1805
Springfield
St Louis
Independence
Pike 1806–7
Arkansas City
Fort Dodge
Tulsa
Arkansas
Memphis
oenix
Santa Fé
Albuquerque
Fremont 1848
Pike 1806–7
Oklahoma City
Little Rock
Fort Worth
Dallas
Jackson
Austin
Houston
New Orleans
San Antonio
Corpus Christi

Pike

Lewis & Clark

Oregon Trail

Santa Fé Trail

Fremont

Mormon Spanish Trail

California Trail

referring to what came to be called the South Pass through the Rockies. In the ensuing years two main trails led into the West: the Oregon Trail going into the north west, the Santa Fe Trail leading to the Old Spanish Trail and the south west. Both started out at St Louis on the Mississippi, or a little further west at St Joseph or Independence on the Missouri.

Many went on foot with their cattle and a pack horse or two in tow, using rafts and flat-boats to travel up the wide Missouri. But for those making the two-thousand mile journey to the Far West, the best vehicle seems to have been the covered wagon, a modified version of the Conestoga Wagon. Both vehicles have been called the 'prairie schooner' at one time or another, but the phrase seems more appropriate for the high-flying ends of the Conestoga than for the more stolid straight ends of the settlers' wagons. Blacksmiths, saddlers and gunsmiths in places like St Louis, St Joseph and Independence were kept busy repairing if not making the heavy wagons, shoeing horses and oxen and outfitting the defenders of the wagon trains.

In his novel *The Pioneers*, James Fenimore Cooper notes, 'people often laid aside the axe or the scythe to seize the rifle as the deer glided through the forests they were felling or the bear entered their rough meadows to scent the air of a clearing and to scan with a look of sagacity the progress of the invader.' Francis Parkman would later have added that the ambitious tenderfoot, though the proud possessor of a Winchester with sixteen cartridges in its magazine, would still be advised to go warily when confronted by a grizzly, even

70. Wrought iron gold miner's candle-holder or 'sticking tommy' as the miners called them, probably made by a local blacksmith in Columbia, California in the late 1860s.

71. Steel candleholder or 'sticking tommy' said to have been used in the Gold King Mine where the Cripple Creek vein—one of the world's most renowned gold deposits in Colorado—was discovered in 1859.

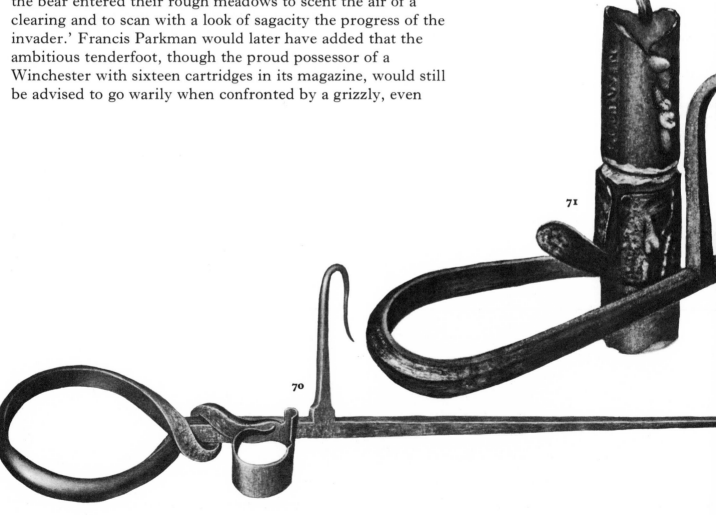

72. A peavey—an American invention named after John—or was it Joseph?—Peavey, the blacksmith who is said to have invented it in 1870 when according to one authority he made one tool out of the cant hook used for rolling logs and the jam pike used for prying them. This one was probably made about 1870 in Wisconsin. Lumbermen by the thousands swarmed into Wisconsin, Michigan and Illinois during a lumber boom which began in the 1820s and lasted almost a century.

though its ferocious strength was no match for the repeating rifle.

The most famous American rifle in use in the late 18th and early 19th centuries was a long rifle, known variously as the Pennsylvania or the Kentucky rifle. It is thought to have been invented in the Lancaster area of eastern Pennsylvania about the middle of the 18th century when a number of expert gunsmiths are known to have been working in the area. Lancaster was a fur-trading depot at the time so there was a ready market for firearms, and excellent bar iron and gunstock timber were easy to come by. Incorporating the suggestions of experienced riflemen and the experiments of numerous artisans, the German Jaeger or hunting rifle was transformed into its American incarnation, the barrel lengthened to improve accuracy, the bore reduced for economy of powder and ball, the trigger guard made sturdier, and balance improved, the sights better designed, and most important, the ball made smaller than the bore and encased with a greased cloth, which made for faster loading and imparted spin to the bullet.

One of the first efficient revolvers was produced by Samuel Colt in 1836. The Winchester 1873 was one of the more famous repeating rifles.

In describing the privations of the early settlers in Michigan, which became a state in 1837, the author of a series of articles in *Godey's Lady's Book* in the 1850s said, 'not least of [the privations] . . . was the difficulty of hearing from the friends they had left in the East. Not only was the mail slow and uncertain, but the postage of a letter was 25¢—a fourth of a

72

75. In 1848, a *Handbook for Settlers in the United States* said of the axe, 'this implement so essential to the settlers in our woods, has here been perfected to a high degree. Its curved edge, its heavier head, counterbalanced by the handle, gives the axe greater power in its swing, facilitates its penetration, reduces the expenditure of human energy, speeds up the work . . .' In the 1870s visiting museum directors began to think that 'a display of American axes could be the source of esthetic delight as strong as an actual work of art'. Shelburne Museum, Vermont.

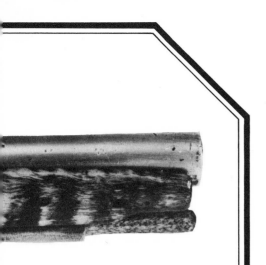

73. American flintlock pistol 1770–80, marked Jacob Grubb. Winchester Gun Museum, New Haven, Connecticut.

74. A log measure and caliper. Shelburne Museum, Vermont.

man's pay for a hard day's work. So expensive a treat could not be often indulged in.' A visiting English correspondent some years earlier had noted that all the stage coaches running in the interior carried the mail and that 'Government contracts which make any mention of time give it in days and not in shabby hours and minutes'. Things looked up a bit in the Far West, at any rate, with the institution of the Pony Express in 1860, a relay system of some seventy-five speedy horse (despite the title) riders, who could get a letter from St Joseph, Missouri, to Sacramento, California, in eight to nine days, two weeks faster than the Overland Mail. But this dashing and daring enterprise was defeated, after a short eighteen-month or so existence, by the installation of telegraph lines to California in 1861. The stage coaches also fell into disuse after the completion of the transcontinental railway in 1869.

Bridge toll tokens, said to be the oldest type of transportation token, are a particular specialty in Pennsylvania, where 52 of the 168 varieties known today are to be found. In 1973 the demolition and replacement of the bridge which spanned the Mississippi between Muscatine, Iowa, and a point just south of Rock Island, Illinois, and for eighty-two years provided safe passage for millions of pedestrians and riders on horseback or in Model T Fords, has given a particular sentimental value to the already rare Muscatine Bridge tokens.

The discovery of gold and silver, first in California in 1848, then in Nevada in 1859, and in Colorado in 1859 and 1890—to mention only four of the biggest rushes—lured a veritable flood of adventurers into the West, intending to make their fortunes and get back East fast to spend them, just as many of the first arrivals in the East had intended to get back to the Old Countries a few centuries back. The soaring price of gold on international money markets in the early 1970s has sent prospectors scurrying back to the last big boom town in Colorado, Cripple Creek—cows broke legs trying to cross it— where it is estimated that only something like 27 per cent of the gold to be found in a huge basin, six miles by four miles, was ever mined. Lost treasure stories are, as the saying goes, a dime a dozen. Arizona has its Lost Dutchman Mine, and New Mexico has its Great White Sands Missile Range Lost Treasure Affair. That one has been going on for about thirty-five years and has involved, at one time or another, the Army, the Air Force, the White House, Congressmen, Apache war chiefs, the State Governor, and lawyers and claimants, identified and unidentified, by the score. But Victoria Peak in the San Andres Mountains on the White Sands Missile Range has not yet given up its treasure, if it has, or ever had, any hidden.

One of the few legal ways for United States citizens to own gold is in the form of coins, so with the Stock Market being what it is, gold coin collecting has become one of the fastest-growing hobbies.

An intriguing set of gold coins for those of us marching along the trail are the private issues which appeared on and off over a period of about twelve years, after the discovery of gold in California in 1848, until just before Congress passed a law in 1864 forbidding the issue of gold coins by private individuals. Variously known as necessity coinage, or more romantically as pioneer or territorial gold, these coins were issued by private companies in California, Oregon, Utah and Colorado, in sizes ranging from a small round $2\frac{1}{2}$ piece, to a largish octagonal $50 'slug', although the most common denominations were the $5, $10, and $20 pieces. Estimates on the total value of the coins issued in California alone, vary from as low as $10 million to as high as $50 million. Many, if not most, were probably melted down. A fair number are almost certainly buried with the wrecks of various steamers struggling to get into, or out of, San Francisco, and some few may still be stowed away in safe deposit vaults or in attic trunks. Some still have to be documented. Others, particularly the small denominations—$\frac{1}{4}$, $\frac{1}{2}$ and $1, will perhaps always be objects of mystery, whose makers made a brief appearance and then disappeared without trace.

Favourite California designs show a mounted rider swinging a lariat or lasso, and an independence cap on a pole surrounded by rays and stars. Colorado has its Pike's Peak, the Mormons of Utah a Phrygian crown and an all-seeing eye, and Oregon—appropriately enough for an area whose early riches came from peltries—its 'beavers'. These were all issued by private companies. Neither the States nor the Territorial governments were allowed to coin gold, only the Federal government and—by one of those odd quirks of the law—individuals were. California became a State in 1850, and made many a threat to secede in the ensuing years, because of its quarrels with the Federal government over coinage.

All this private coinage certainly facilitated business and trade in the new lands, once dependent on the older and simpler barter system, but because some were 'irregular in weight and debased in fineness' (denoted on a scale up to one thousand which equalled pure gold) they cast doubt on the whole system. Moreover, the United States Mint in Philadelphia was not very happy about the production of coins 'in imitation of the national coinage'. Branch Mints were opened in San Francisco in 1856, and in Denver, Colorado, in 1862. But early difficulties meant there was still a need for private coins. The Denver Branch did not succeed in starting its operations until 1906. However, since none of the areas seceded when Congress passed its law forbidding private issues of gold coins in 1864, frontier economics were presumably not too seriously dislocated by its passage!

76. Rare early 18th-century glass powder horn thought to have been made in America's first successful glass-house established by Caspar Wistar in New Jersey.

77. History lesson on a powder horn. Many settlers from the United States moved into Texas after the area became part of the Republic of Mexico in 1821. In 1836 they rebelled against Mexican rule and after being defeated at the Alamo managed to establish themselves as an independent republic. In 1845 the United States took the fateful step of annexing Texas and went to war with Mexico to defend its action. The result was that not only Texas but a huge area of other formerly Spanish-held land in the south west became part of the United States and the shape of the continental United States was just about completed.

On the powder flask:

1836

TO LOYALTY A TOAST

TEXICANS UNITE

Asa Good.

78. Spanish Californian ring bit made of wrought iron with silver inlay probably in the Los Angeles area about 1880. A ring bit, sometimes said to be the cruelest ever used, was capable of breaking a horse's jaw.

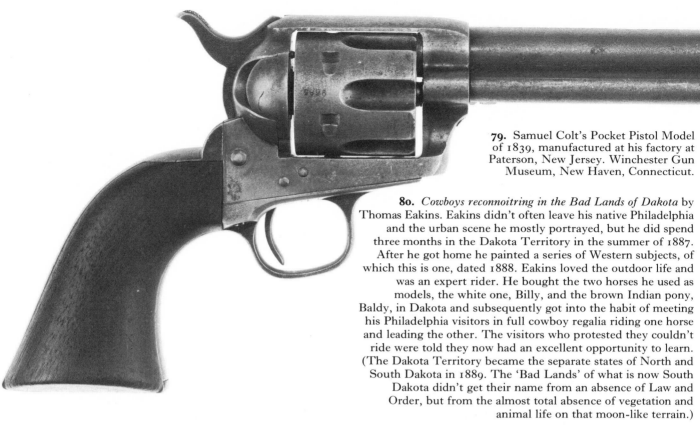

79. Samuel Colt's Pocket Pistol Model of 1839, manufactured at his factory at Paterson, New Jersey. Winchester Gun Museum, New Haven, Connecticut.

80. *Cowboys reconnoitring in the Bad Lands of Dakota* by Thomas Eakins. Eakins didn't often leave his native Philadelphia and the urban scene he mostly portrayed, but he did spend three months in the Dakota Territory in the summer of 1887. After he got home he painted a series of Western subjects, of which this is one, dated 1888. Eakins loved the outdoor life and was an expert rider. He bought the two horses he used as models, the white one, Billy, and the brown Indian pony, Baldy, in Dakota and subsequently got into the habit of meeting his Philadelphia visitors in full cowboy regalia riding one horse and leading the other. The visitors who protested they couldn't ride were told they now had an excellent opportunity to learn. (The Dakota Territory became the separate states of North and South Dakota in 1889. The 'Bad Lands' of what is now South Dakota didn't get their name from an absence of Law and Order, but from the almost total absence of vegetation and animal life on that moon-like terrain.)

81 Smith and Wesson centre-fire revolver, Model 1881. Winchester Gun Museum, New Haven, Connecticut.

82. The famous single-action Army Model of 1873, known as the Frontier Model or the 'Peacemaker'. Winchester Gun Museum, New Haven, Connecticut.

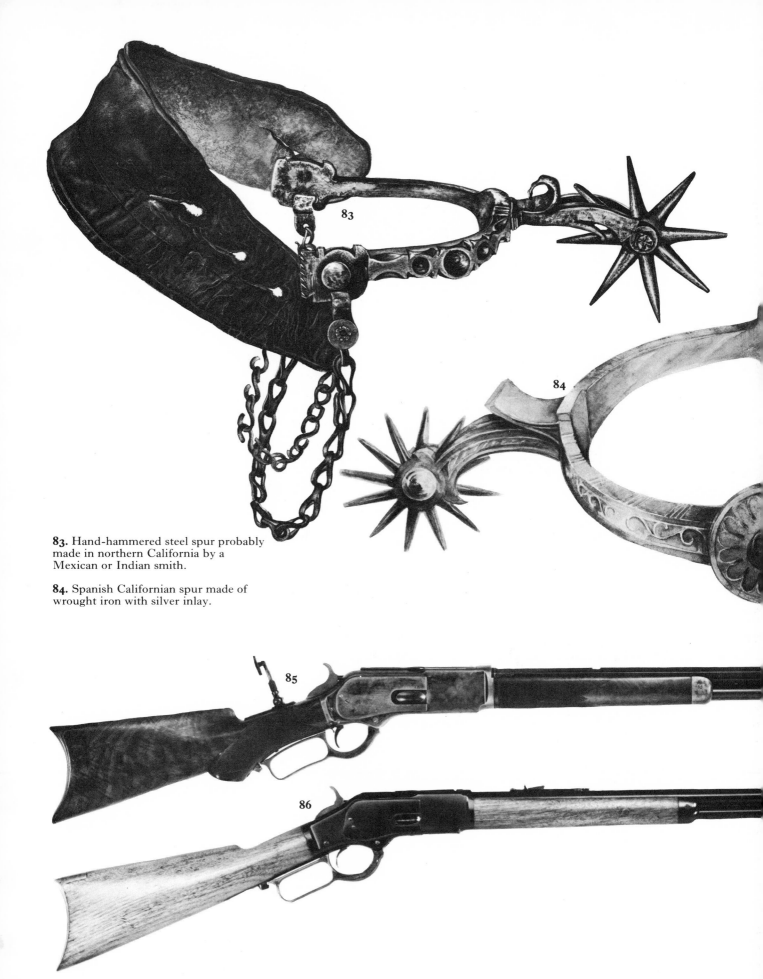

83. Hand-hammered steel spur probably made in northern California by a Mexican or Indian smith.

84. Spanish Californian spur made of wrought iron with silver inlay.

The never-ending struggle between fact and mythology along the trail into the American West, is perhaps nowhere so great as among the cowboys in the Cattle Kingdom that stretched across the Great Plains between the Mississippi and the Rocky Mountains, and from Canada in the north, to the Gulf of Mexico in the south. Drenched as we are in the endless stories of their exploits, it comes as a surprise to learn that the heyday of the cowboy was a brief thirty-year period, from the end of the Civil War in the 1860s, to the end of the century, when barbed wire successfully closed off the open range. The early railways reaching out from the East to places like Chicago and Abilene, Kansas, made possible the annual long drive of cattle along the Chisholm Trail, for example, for entrainment to northern and eastern markets. The later spread of the railways, and the closing of the trails, put an end to that colourful pilgrimage.

Much of the cowboy's equipment and that of his horse, and all other horses and horsemen in the West, derived in name and style from Mexican gear, which of course derived from Spanish and Moorish designs. There are numerous versions of the Western saddle, but all are basically different from the flat English type, which was often referred to contemptuously as a 'pimple' or a 'pancake', or by some other equally slighting term. The sturdy upward projecting pommel at the front of the Western saddle was necessary for lashing rope and the upward curving canticle—that's the back—gave the rider better support. Some stirrups have covers named after the Spanish *tapadera*, but are known more graphically as 'toe fenders', since they only cover the front part of the foot. These were made of leather and were sometimes mounted on a wooden frame. They protected the feet in brush country and prevented them from slipping through the stirrups. The Mountain Man in one of Albert Bierstadt's paintings is wearing a very shaggy pair of buffalo-hide toe fenders. The rider in the painting, *Wild Horses* (page 113), is wearing a leather pair, and the saddle (page 85) also has them. The high heels on cowboy boots also served to prevent feet from slipping through stirrups. Protection and warmth were practical reasons for the height of the boots, most of which were about 17 inches tall. The boots made for cowboy artist Charles Russell, who roamed the range in the last decades of the century, are now in the Justin Boot Collection of the National Cowboy Hall of Fame in Oklahoma City. Many cowboy boots were custom-made and a source of great pride to their owners, who, it seems, were quite vain about having small feet! Rawhide chaps (from the Spanish *chaparreras*) saved pants and legs from being ripped to shreds in prickly pear country, among impenetrable thickets of mesquite and many another thorny growth. The fringes on rawhide jackets served their purpose in a rainstorm by carrying away some of

85. An extra fine quality Model 1876 Winchester, said to be perfect in every respect. Winchester Gun Museum, New Haven, Connecticut.

86. The Model 1873 Winchester repeater designed for centre-fire cartridges and made in various calibres. Winchester Gun Museum, New Haven, Connecticut.

87. Settlers' wagons like this one, big enough for a whole family and all its household goods, moved out along the trails beyond the Mississippi in trains of six to eight into what is sometimes called the Real West.

No. 2, the "Cleveland Barbed Wire." The points stand out at nearly right angles, which could not well be shown in the engrav-

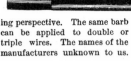

ing perspective. The same barb can be applied to double or triple wires. The names of the manufacturers unknown to us.

No. 3.—Engraved from a specimen; distinctive name unknown. These barbs also stand out at

right angles, that is, in four directions. We are not aware that this form is now being manufactured.

No. 4, the "Kelly Steel Barb Wire," with the two-point barb stamped or cut from sheet metal, and pierced to string upon one

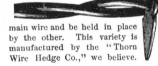

main wire and be held in place by the other. This variety is manufactured by the "Thorn Wire Hedge Co.," we believe.

No. 5, "Roberts Barbed Wire," engraved from specimen; if now manufactured, the makers are as yet unknown to us. The two-pointed barb is

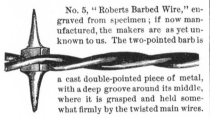

a cast double-pointed piece of metal, with a deep groove around its middle, where it is grasped and held somewhat firmly by the twisted main wires.

No. 6, the "Crandall's Barbed Wire," is simple, and this barb may probably be put upon a single wire, like No. 2, but when there are only

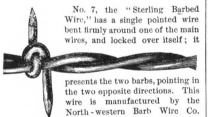

two barbs, they need to be set closer together than for the four barbs. Made by the Chicago Galvanizing Co.

No. 7, the "Sterling Barbed Wire," has a single pointed wire bent firmly around one of the main wires, and locked over itself; it

presents the two barbs, pointing in the two opposite directions. This wire is manufactured by the North-western Barb Wire Co.

No. 8, the "Bronson Barbed Wire." The two barbs are

formed by cutting one of the running wires, and bending and locking the ends. We do not know the manufacturers.

No. 9—The "Glidden Steel Barbed Fencing." The barb has a close double turn around one of the main wires.

To reduce the objections to dangerous points, this variety has for some time past been made with the barbs materi-

ally shortened. Manufactured by the Washburn & Moen M'f'g. Co., as per advertisement elsewhere.

No. 10, the "Three-pointed, Stone City Steel Barbed

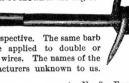

Wire," has a 3-pointed piece locked between the two main wires. Made by the Stone City Barb Wire Fence Co.

No. 11. "The Steel Barbed Cable Fence," (Frentress' & Scutt's patents), is similar to No. 10, but with 4 barbs

on one solid piece. Made by the Illinois Fence Company. Two other barbs, somewhat similar to these, are made by H. B. Scutt & Co.

No. 12. "Spiral Twist, 4-pointed, Steel-barbed Cable Fence Wire"

(Watkins' patent). The barbs are on one solid piece of metal, which is bent to conform to the twist of the main wires, and is thus held fast. Made by Watkins & Ashley.

No. 13, the "Quadrated Barbed Fence," is explained by the engraving. It has well-fastened barbs certainly. Made, we believe, by Pittsburgh Hinge Co.

No. 14. The "Iowa 4-pointed Barbed Steel Wire," (Burnell's patent). The form and structure are plainly shown in the

engraving. The wire of the barbs passes twice around and between the main wires, but so loosely as to yield a little. It is made by the Iowa Barb Steel Wire Co., both in Iowa and New York, as advertised elsewhere.

No. 15. We give the name "Lyman Manufacturing Co. Barbed Fence" to this, from

the Company reported as manufacturing it. Its form is shown in the engraving.

No. 16. The "Allis Patent Barb," is all the name we have heard for this. Our specimen is a solid

piece of the form shown in the engraving herewith.

No. 17, the "American Barb Fence." A central, wire closely sheathed with a continuous metal strip, with its edges cut in the form of barbs, turned out in all directions, the points one inch apart. The

whole is covered and saturated with paint or zinc, firmly cementing the outer and inner metal. Made by the American Barb Fence Co., (J. C. Taylor, General Agent), as advertised elsewhere.

84

88. Barbed wire examples from the *American Agriculturist*, January 1880. Barbed wire, thought to be the last word in fencing when it was first being used in the 1860s and 1870s turned out to be the second last—replaced towards the end of the century by among other things woven wire fencing. Today the numerous varieties of 'bobbed' wire as it's called in Texas or 'devil's rope' as it was sometimes called, have become collectors' items.

89. Child's side saddle made by an unknown craftsman at Monterey, California about 1820.

90. Hand-tooled leather side saddle with white felt seat thought to have been made in the mid 19th century on a ranch in the Santa Barbara area at a time when the long line of Missions from San Diego in the south to San Francisco in the north—the centres of much excellent craft work in the last flowering of Spanish Colonial and then Mexican rule in the late 18th and early 19th centuries—were in decline.

91. *Crossing the Rockies*. Coloured lithograph by Currier & Ives, New York, second half of the 19th century. The American Museum in Britain, Bath.

the water. The wide bronc-buster's belt gave support to the back and the abdomen of the rider, who broke or bust the spirit of a bronc, bronco (Spanish *broncho*) or wild horse. The sombrero or ten-gallon hat—it *was* sometimes used as a bucket, although it may not always have held 10 gallons—kept sun and wind out of the eyes, and because of its deep crown stayed firmly on the head even at full gallop after a stampeding herd. Rope, the cowboy's most important tool, now mostly made of nylon, was once made of horsehair or from a Mexican plant called henequen.

Many an eye-brow is raised when the conversation gets around to barbed wire, and yet I hazard the guess that there are actually more varieties of this mass-produced texture than there are of spurs and saddles, boots and sombreros. I have not counted them, of course, but no doubt somebody will.

The first patents on barbed wire were taken out in 1867, but it was not until 1874, when Joseph Glidden of De Kalb, Illinois, invented a practical machine for mass-producing it, that the industry really got under way. There are only a few standard types of barbed wire. It is in fact, nothing more than two strands of wire twisted to form a cable, having wire barbs with points cut diagonally for sharpness wound around either one or both cable wires at regular intervals. But the combinations and permutations of wire type and gauge, spacing differences and varieties of barbs, put the possible types in the five to six hundred region. Flat wire with a serrated edge is not barbed wire. It is rather decorative but was easily broken. Cattle running against it, or just leaning against it, would do the trick, and so would a little expansion and contraction in hot and cold weather. That is one reason why they decided they needed two wires in the barbed variety—they could expand and contract without snapping.

The range had been open and free because fencing materials were scarce on the vast, treeless prairies and plains, and the cost of hauling wood from the East prohibitive. Barbed wire was the first cheap substitute for wooden fences. It caused fierce range wars between ranchers and homesteaders, or 'nesters', as the cowboys called the latest wave of settlers in the West who took advantage of Lincoln's Homestead Act and the railways' offer of cheap, if not always cultivateable, land. They lived in a 'little old sod shanty on my claim' as the song goes, and were sodbusters in the way cowboys were sometimes bronco-busters.

In 1892 Francis Parkman noted, 'The buffalo is gone and of all his millions nothing is left but bones. Tame cattle and fences of barbed wire have supplanted his vast herd and boundless grazing grounds. . . .'

The title of an exhibition of American paintings held at New York's Whitney Museum in 1973 was 'The American Frontier—Images and Myths'. It was a clear case of History

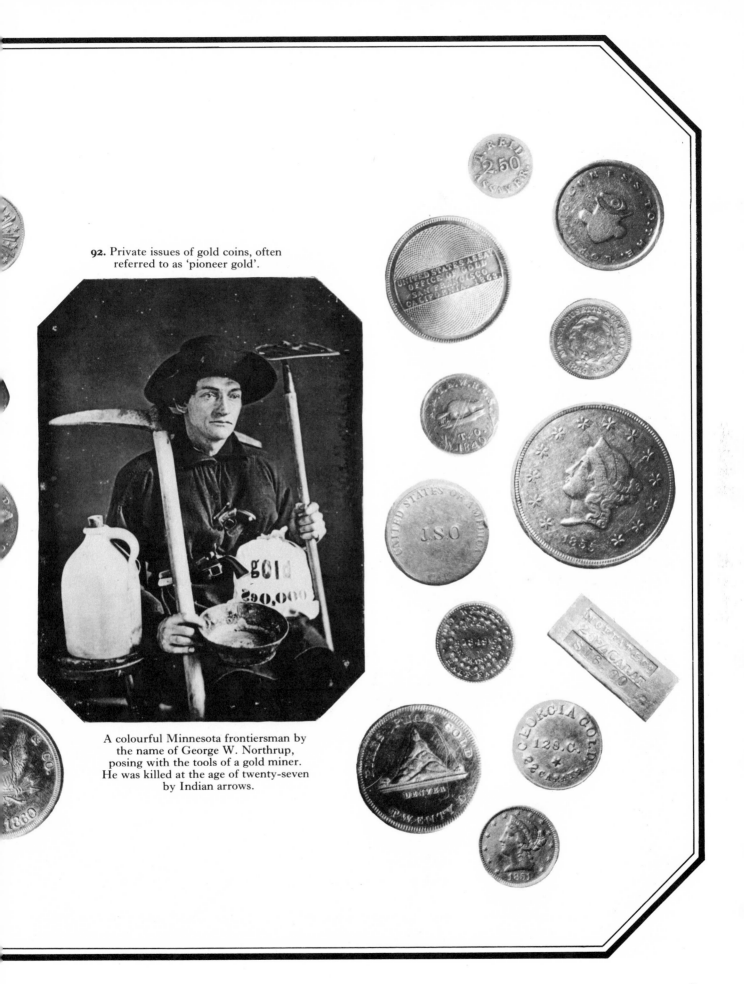

92. Private issues of gold coins, often referred to as 'pioneer gold'.

A colourful Minnesota frontiersman by the name of George W. Northrup, posing with the tools of a gold miner. He was killed at the age of twenty-seven by Indian arrows.

triumphing over Art, or as one expert put it . . . 'sociohistorical rather than esthetic in focus'. The paintings were not very good in themselves, but were fascinating as stories. And the main line of the story they told was that the frontier was the boundary between civilisation and savagery; that explorers and plainsmen were well-scrubbed demigods in coonskin caps; that the pioneers—traders, farmers, miners, ranchers—were heroic figures upholding the doctrine of Manifest Destiny which required that they convert the New Land into their own Promised Land, and that the Indians were savage marauders, killers of wagon-trains full of young mothers and infants.

Before about 1820, artists illustrating the journals of explorers and historians relied on hearsay and imagination, but after about that time, artists were lured along the trail like many another. They became part of official expeditions, accompanied explorers and surveyors; or just went off to see for themselves, and document what they saw, or thought they saw. In the 1830s, James Otto Lewis was commissioned by the Department of Indian Affairs to attend council meetings with Indian chiefs, make portraits of the chiefs, and depict the various events surrounding the meetings during which treaties were made and millions of acres of rich agricultural land

93 (pages 90–91). *Cowboy Fun in Old Mexico* painted by Frederick Remington, a Yale football star who went west in search of adventure and fortune. With enough money to do as he pleased, 'Sackrider' Remington rode all the old trails from Canada to Old Mexico, determined to know the story of the Old West better than anyone else. He talked to old-timers, visited Indian camps, prospected for gold, joined United States cavalry units and fought in the last Indian War. He also taught himself to paint. Within three years after his return to New York in 1885 he was doing all the Western illustrations for the country's top magazines.

94. *Midnight Race on the Mississippi*— lithograph by Currier & Ives. Rising in Minnesota just south of the Canadian border and flowing south for more than two thousand miles into the Gulf of Mexico, the Mississippi was the new Republic's first western frontier in 1783. In the 19th century the steamboat solved the problem of upstream navigation and turned New Orleans into sugar and cotton capital of North America.

95. *The Express Train*—lithograph by Currier & Ives. A correspondent for a London magazine in the late 1830s noted, 'Railroads . . . are making rapid inroads upon the canal traffic; and when we take into the account both the extent and general levelness of the country, there is no saying where they may terminate—probably at the foot of the Rocky Mountains, or on the shores of the Pacific.' The first railway spanning the continent was completed in 1869. Currier & Ives, Printmakers to the American People, as they called themselves, outdid all rivals in capturing in their coloured engravings the whole panorama of American life in the latter part of the 19th century from the elegant crowd in the urban east to the simple joys of country life and the constant push west. An estimated ten million prints with some seven thousand different titles were produced. An Englishwoman immigrant was the work-horse artist who did most of the original drawings for the lithographers.

96 (pages 94–95). *When the Trail was Long and Hard between Camps*, 1901. Charles Marion Russell, watercolour and gouache.

purchased. Alfred Jacob Miller went with William Drummond Stewart, a Scotsman who was among the numerous foreign explorers who mounted expeditions into the interior, and Miller consequently had the good fortune to be present at the Green River rendez-vous in 1837—the only artist known to have made on-the-spot drawings of the annual get-together of trappers and traders. George Catlin, generally considered the first artist of real stature to go into the West, also went under his own steam, so to speak, and concentrated on Indians. But pre-eminent among the graphic chroniclers of the Old West were in a sense the last two: Frederick Remington and Charles Russell, who in the late 19th century went off on their own and recorded the last of the wagon-trains, the mounted cavalry units, the great herds of long horns and the tumult of the buffalo stampede, the hard-riding cowboys, the taciturn mountain men, prospectors and Indians, gamblers and law-men, the whole long list of characters who participated in the drama of the trail. And even if that drama is being more critically appraised nowadays—more universities are offering courses on the American frontier than ever before—it is unlikely that it will ever loose all of the romantic aura that has grown around it. Some of it was real!

Folk Artist

SAMUEL Morse, inventor of the telegraph, inveterate explorer and visionary tinkerer, who made his daughter and her friend pose for ten to twenty minutes in bright sun, with their eyes closed and their heads held steady with a clamp, while he and a chemist friend, John William Draper, took what is thought to be the first American portrait with a camera, had, in his youth, wanted to be a portrait painter. He was awarded the coveted commission to paint the official portrait of the French General Lafayette, when that friend of the Republic made a triumphant visit in 1824. But when Morse was searching for more humble commissions in rural New England, he dolefully announced: 'The quacks got here before me'.

The great period of the quacks or, to be a little more polite than Morse, the self-taught, itinerant artists or naive limners, as they are often called, who painted the farmers and tradesmen and their families, the inn signs and the landscapes, and persuaded housewives to buy them along with the more practical wares they were peddling, is thought to coincide roughly with the first fifty years or so of the New Republic, from about 1785 to 1840. Not many operated west of the Mississippi, although San Francisco became a new centre of inspiration around the middle of the 19th century.

These largely anonymous artists – essentially artisans

97. Sign Shop, Guthrie, Oklahoma Territory, 1889. Temporary wooden offices and shops were thrown up shortly after a big land run into Oklahoma. Western History Collections, University of Oklahoma Library, Norman.

98. Unique life-sized great blue heron made by noted decoy-maker A. Elmer Crowell probably as a display piece never destined to see service in the marshes on raw autumn days. The heron was one of the birds hunted primarily for its feathers and mostly in the coastal regions of Long Island and New Jersey.

99. Carved wooden shop sign-cum-weathervane for a slaughterhouse probably made about 1850. Interestingly enough, systematic teamwork, the precursor of assembly-line production and the beginnings of a meat industry of continental proportions, is thought to have started with the killing and dressing of hogs in the great slaughterhouses of Cincinnati on the Ohio River in the 1830s. But despite the flood of patents for the necessary machines, many from Cincinnati inventors, no machine has yet been invented that will sever a ham from the carcass of a pig without a little help from a butcher!

100. *Suffragettes Taking the Constitution for a Ride*—painting in the Webb Gallery at the Shelburne Museum. Shelburne Museum, Vermont.

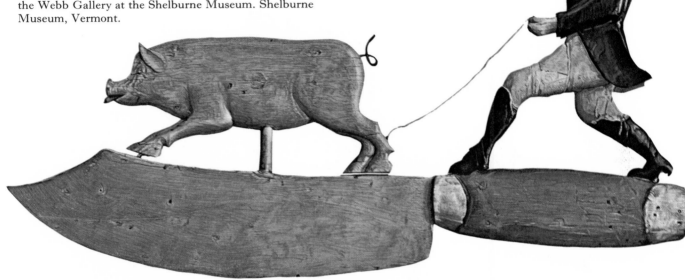

101. *The Peaceable Kingdom* by Edward Hicks, 1780–1849.

skilled in one or other of the crafts—turned to painting in the
summer months as an additional source of income. They did
not know much, if anything, about perspective or anatomy.
They employed ingenious devices to hide difficult-to-paint
hands and were not too good at composition. In fact, they
were conspicuously lacking in technical proficiency. Yet their
best efforts have vitality and freshness and bold, individualistic
imagery uninhibited by academic precepts, and according to
the *Oxford Companion to Art* are 'simple, mannered, but often
ingeniously designed'. For one of the major early collectors of
these paintings the word is 'naive'. This word was adopted in
both the French and the English title of the exhibition of his
collection, which was seen in several European cities in 1968
and 1969 and, as mentioned earlier, is said to have gone a long
way to changing the image of America's past in European eyes.

Portraits—the rent-money of artists for centuries, until
the camera took over—are among the most numerous of the
known folk paintings. The theory that our travelling artists
took along with them stock figures, usually painted in oil on
canvas or wood, to which they just added a head on
commission, is discounted by experts on the grounds that no

Isabella - Maria Wilson fecit / June 28 1826.

102. Still life painting on velvet signed by Isabella Maria Wilson and dated 1826.

headless torsos have ever come to light among collectors' finds, and that it would have been too difficult for the itinerants to look after the partially finished canvases on the road.

Even the greatest artists are known to repeat themselves, so it is not surprising to find artists of limited experience using the same poses, costumes and accessories on more than one occasion.

In the early years of the 19th century, the father of Matthew Harris Jouett who was quite a successful portrait painter, was not all impressed by his son's choice of career: 'I sent Matthew to college to make a gentleman of him' he said, 'and he has turned out to be nothing but a damned sign painter'.

That acute observer of the natural scene, John James Audubon, once observed 'almost every country inn has a Martin-box on the upper part of its sign-board . . . [and] the handsomer the box, the better does the inn generally prove to be'. The inn-keepers seemed to have borrowed an idea from the Indians, who hung hollowed-out gourds at the entrance to their camps for the martins who then chased off any vultures thinking to share the Indians' venison. The coach-painter

102. Still life painting on velvet signed by Isabella Maria Wilson and dated 1826.

103. Dancing girl from Spark's Circus Wagon thought to have been made about 1900 in Wisconsin.

104. A 19th-century carved wooden shop sign for a nautical instrument-maker showing a navigator 'shooting the sun'. In *Dombey and Son* Charles Dickens mentions similar English figures, 'little timber midshipmen in obsolete naval uniforms eternally employed . . . in taking observance of the hackney-coaches'.

105. A 19th-century carved wooden shop sign—a Scotsman taking a pinch of snuff instead of the better known Indian figures used to advertise tobacco.

Fritz Schriber, who worked for the Abbot-Downing Co. of Concord, New Hampshire, where Wells Fargo stage coaches were made for the cross country routes, is said to have exhorted his apprentices to paint the letters big so they could be read when the coach was moving. Would that some of our city buses had passed through his hands!

Among the most notable of the early landscape painters who worked for some time as a sign painter, was Edward Hicks, a Quaker preacher strongly influenced by the evangelical religious movement sweeping through the country in the early part of the 19th century. Hicks painted several Pennsylvania landscapes of serene beauty, but is perhaps best known for one painting, *The Peaceable Kingdom*, of which he did numerous versions. In most of them there is a vignette of William Penn's treaty with the Indians, copied from the academically trained Benjamin West, who had gone off to make his name in London. Penn actually negotiated a series of treaties with Indian tribes after his arrival in Pennsylvania in 1682. West's painting of one of them is considered something of 'an exercise in historical imagination'. Hicks believed that America was the Peaceable Kingdom, that Penn's holy experiment was as close as human kind had come to heaven on earth, and that even animals who are natural enemies would eventually lie down together in harmony. But as one critic has pointed out, Hick's dream was only one prt of the American Dream and it was in conflict with the other part: the Horatio Alger concept of economic success through free enterprise, which had even in Hick's time, changed the American landscape into something different from the unspoiled and heavenly scene he painted. Thirty years ago, one long-time collector is said to have turned down a splendid version of the Peaceable Kingdom because at $500 it was priced 'insanely high'. Today experts conjecture that the same painting would fetch between $125,000 and $175,000 and that long-time collector says, 'No price is too high for something that is absolutely great'. I wonder?

Other identified folk artists are Erastus S. Field, whose *Garden of Eden* is said to show the beauty and abundance of the Connecticut River Valley despite the fanciful nature of much of the flora and fauna he put in it, and Joshua Johnson, the first known American negro portrait painter, who worked in the Baltimore area in the early years of the 19th century. John Bellamy and Joseph Pickett are often talked about in the same breath as Hicks, but some are simply identified by the names of the people they painted, as, for example, the Beardsley limner, some of whose work–*Mr & Mrs B*, for example–is now in Yale University's Art Gallery. The names and work of other artists are gradually being identified as more research is done.

Wall-paper was scarce and expensive in the early

106 & 107. Portraits of John and Polly Fonda, signed by John Wilkie and dated 1839. The artist was kinder to the husband than to the wife or perhaps just found it easier to paint men than women, a not unusual phenomenon, it seems.

19th century, so our friendly travelling artists would
paint the plaster walls with stencilled or freehand repeating
patterns, or decorative scenes, or some topical subject of local
interest. Sam Patch, the man who leapt over, or into, waterfalls,
Niagara included, was found giving an exhibition on a wall in
one New York house. And the sad story of the traitor, Major
Andre, Benedict Arnold's accomplice in purveying military
secrets to the British during the War of Independence, is just
visible on a barn wall now at the American Museum in Britain.

Among the amateur folk artists of the 18th and 19th
centuries were not a few women, for whom the rudiments of
art were a prerequisite for a genteel education. Many used
stencils, called 'theorems' in the instruction books. Still-lifes
were part of the amateur repertoire, as were 'mourning'
pictures—a sometimes strange combination of needlework and
watercolours that always included tombs, weeping willows,
urns and mourning figures, and a lake or pond, or river of

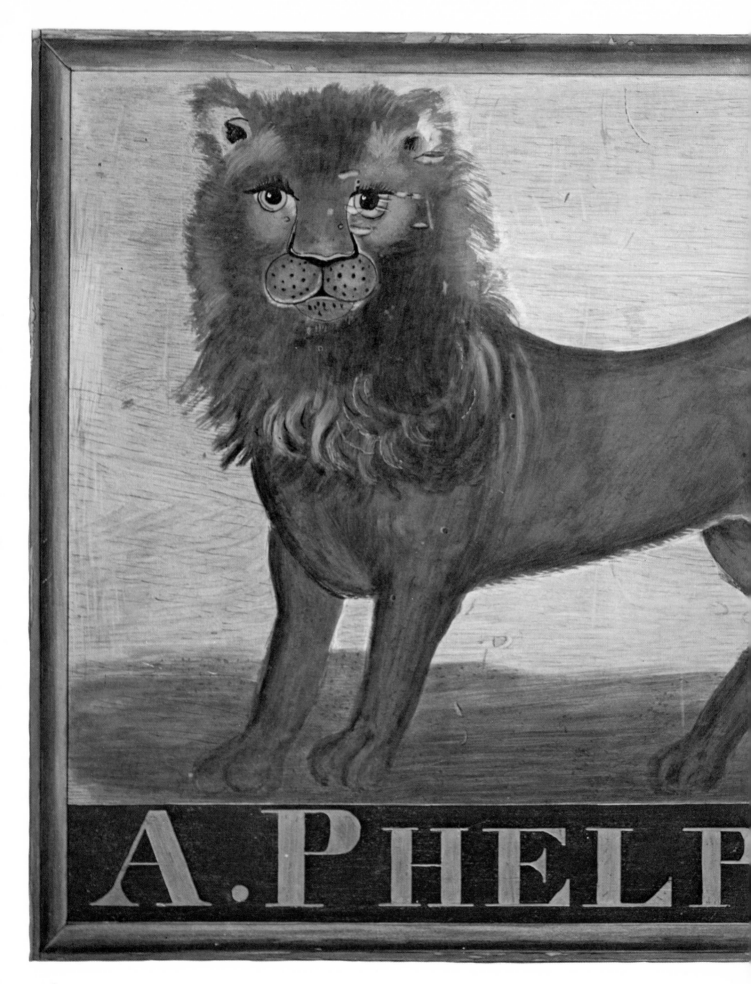

108. Painted tavern sign, identified as the work of an itinerant signpainter called William Rice, who worked in Rhode Island and Connecticut in the 1830s and 1840s.

Rice.

S' INN.

tears. Various other types of pictures were executed in similar media.

A quite special kind of folk painting was done in Pennsylvania, where the primarily German immigrants continued their practice of illuminating family documents—certificates of birth, baptism, marriage and death—religious texts and house blessings, teaching sheets and merit awards, and an occasional love token, which might be no more than a paper cut-out of hearts, decorated in watercolours with other traditional motifs. All of this decorative work is called *Fraktur*, a contraction of *Frakturschrift*—writing, or more appropriately calligraphy that resembled a 16th-century type-face called *Fraktur*. The most popular motifs are conventionalised floral arrangements, with the tulip predominating and variously interpreted as denoting the Trinity of Father, Son and Holy Ghost; a variation of the holy lily and a promise of paradise. Others are the heart, signifying the heart of God and the source of love and hope; the pomegranate, borrowed from Persian textiles by German printers as early as the 12th century; the Tree of Life, with all sorts of birds perched on the branches and leaves and flowers of a wide variety of species; and other

109. Shaker 'inspirational' drawing made by Eldress Polly Reed of Mount Lebanon, New York. The 'inspired' Shaker or 'instrument' did not always do the drawing. If they had no talent in that direction, they simply gave their thoughts to an artist.

human and animal figures, angels and cherubs. Many were
executed by local schoolmasters, ministers, or itinerant artists.
Some are signed, others are simply identified by a recurring
motif, such as 'the cross-legged angel'. The earliest are thought
to have been done in Ephrata, Pennsylvania, about 1730.
Towards the end of the century, the text portion was produced
by the printing press, not by hand, as previously.

After painting comes sculpture, even in folk art, and
that means that the first most interesting pieces of folk
sculpture are the figureheads which, once again, were made
mostly in the seaports of the East coast. Guardian spirit of
ships since ancient times, the figurehead in its American
incarnation—that is, after Independence—inclined to broad
planes and large contours, rather than elaborate detail. It was
usually made of pine, a soft wood which is easily cut and
chiselled, and then painted or gilded. Apart from the prow
where the figurehead stood, the stern of a ship was another
popular candidate for decoration. Three different types of
ships carried these decorations throughout the 19th century:
the whalers, the clipper ships and the steam-boats. And the

110. *Old Kentucky Home; Life in the
South*, 1859. Eastman Johnson 1824–
1906, oil on canvas, New-York
Historical Society, New York City.

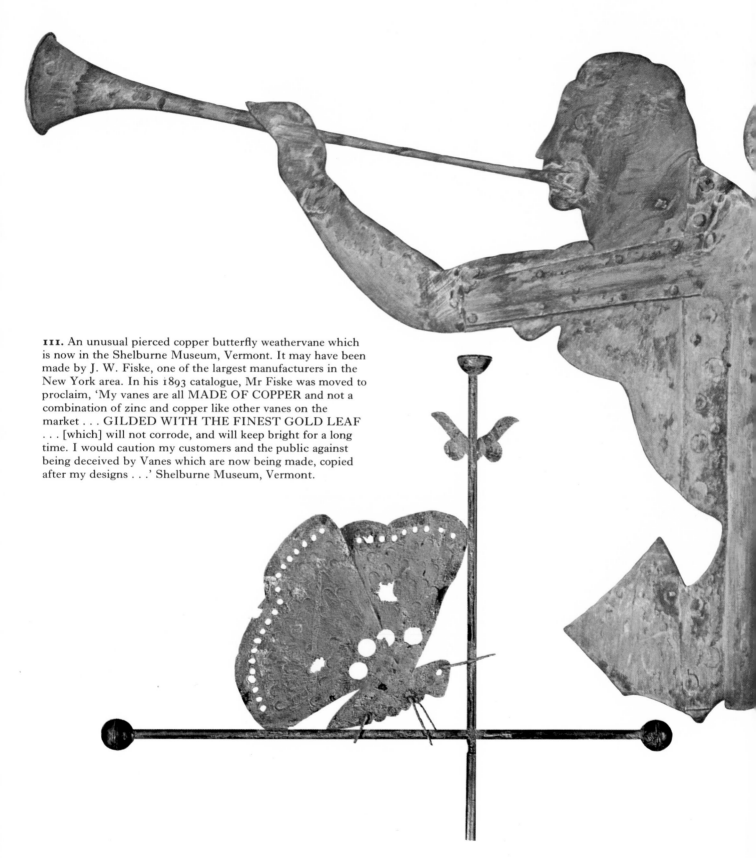

III. An unusual pierced copper butterfly weathervane which is now in the Shelburne Museum, Vermont. It may have been made by J. W. Fiske, one of the largest manufacturers in the New York area. In his 1893 catalogue, Mr Fiske was moved to proclaim, 'My vanes are all MADE OF COPPER and not a combination of zinc and copper like other vanes on the market . . . GILDED WITH THE FINEST GOLD LEAF . . . [which] will not corrode, and will keep bright for a long time. I would caution my customers and the public against being deceived by Vanes which are now being made, copied after my designs . . .' Shelburne Museum, Vermont.

112. The Archangel Gabriel as weathervane—the shapely, gilded iron body blowing a tubular copper trumpet was made by Gould & Hazlett of Boston in 1840. The feminine curves produced startled comment some years ago when this water-colour rendering of the original was used on a postage stamp.

quality of their figureheads and stern carvings are sometimes rated in the same order. Most characteristic of the New Bedford and Nantucket whalers are the portraits of the shipowner's wife or daughter decorously dressed in her Sunday-go-to-meeting best. The carvings on the clipper ships, appropriately enough for ships designed for speed, are more glamorous, but still shaped, according to Henry Wadsworth Longfellow in his poem, *The Building of the Ship*,

> . . . not . . . in the classic mould,
> Not like a Nymph or Goddess of old,
> Or Naïad rising from the water,
> But modelled from the Master's daughter.

Other subjects, however, such as Indian maids and chiefs, allegorical figures, characters from literature, men of the day, or Columbia, the American Goddess of Liberty and others of her kind, were also popular on the clipper ships. And there were eagles, eagles, everywhere, in an infinite variety of perches, poses and positions. The delicate and slow process of sifting out the more sophisticated work by craftsmen such as William Rush—whose Indian Trader for the ship called the *William Penn* created quite a stir when it arrived at the London docks—from the more primitive work, and the more vital primitive work from the more pedestrian, is still going on. The age of Steam is said to mark the decline of the figurehead. In 1907 the Navy ordered the removal of figureheads from all ships of the fleet, and in a rhyme of the day,

> . . . the art is gone for the War Ship of steel
> Is a barren stretch the length of her keel;
> From her tier of guns to the waterline red
> With never the sign of a figurehead.

By that time, however, many ships' carvers had turned away from a diminishing business and were working in a more thriving area on shop and tavern signs.

Nobody has yet determined when and where cigar-store Indians first appeared. The first English examples, called 'Black Boys', seem to have figured on the streets of London early in the 18th century. They were rather hybrid in character, with something in them of the Indian who first smoked tobacco, the negro slave who harvested it, and the Virginian who exported it. The heyday for the American examples is the latter half of the 19th century. They are mostly made of white pine, but some were made of cast iron, which was more expensive but had the advantage of being a little too heavy for thieves to carry away. One New York firm advertised pewter and zinc Indians towards the end of the century. Some itinerant painters actually managed to make a full-time business out of repainting cigar-store figures.

Among the American examples, Indians—braves and squaws—predominate to give the shop sign its generic name, but where the earliest carvers got their models remains a mystery. The consensus is that George Catlin's lithographic gallery was probably the one and only source of authentic reference easily available to them, and that most carvers relied more on the romantic images found in popular prints, and the novels of James Fenimore Cooper, for example. Among the male figures are scouts, shielding their eyes with their hands, hunters with tomahawks, axes, guns, and bows and arrows, and sometimes even a rare trapper. Among the non-Indian figures are those of Sir Walter Raleigh, a Turk, a Scots Highlander, Punch, Uncle Sam, Miss Liberty, and from the end of the 19th century all sorts of dudes and dandies, Rough Riders, and Admiral Dewey. One of the earliest and most

113. Beaten copper weathervane made about the middle of the 18th century by Shem Drowne, the earliest known American maker of weathervanes.

114. *Wild Horses* by Charles Ostner, who may or may not have been the Charles Hinkley Ostner listed as a sculptor and carver active in San Francisco from 1856–9. Horses were re-introduced into the New World by Hernando Cortez and the conquistadors early in the 16th century and were an indispensable part of life here for at least the next four centuries. As the saying went, 'A man afoot is no man at all'.

original female figures, now in the New York Historical Association's Museum at Cooperstown, New York, is thought to be the work of a New Jersey negro craftsman. Few craftsmen actually signed or dated their work, although one or two notable pieces have been attributed to Julius Theodore Melchers, an immigrant Danish ships' carver who worked in Detroit. Many of the figures produced in such States as Wisconsin, Illinois and Michigan, are thought to be the work of immigrant German, Swiss and Danish craftsmen. It is believed that of the estimated 75,000 figures produced in the second half of the 19th century, only a few thousand have survived. At the end of the century they were branded as traffic obstructions and ordered off the sidewalks. One collector believes that there is scarcely a typical character that has not been immortalised in advertising a tobacco shop. Indians and others all held out or on to cigars, snuff, tobacco-leaves, or a tobacco-box, as the specific symbols of the trade, although after a while the figures themselves became so well established that the tobacco details were of little importance, at least to shoppers in the late 19th century.

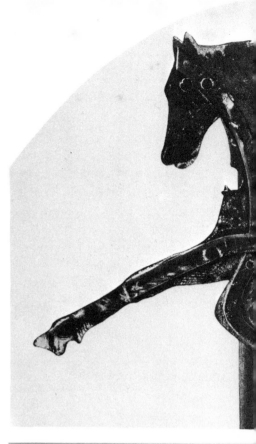

Other tradesmen to use graphic, fully rounded, free-swinging symbols in the days before universal literacy, and long before the tobacconist got hold of the idea, were the apothecary, the shoemaker, the hatter, the joiner, the cabinetmaker, the barber, the tanner, the grain dealer, the butcher, the baker, the candlestick-maker, and the tavern-keeper too, before the painted signboard displaced all the symbols. A handsome boot, a dinosaur-sized tooth, a pair of spectacles, a manacled felon, told a story faster than any words could, in fact, transcended all languages. This could be one reason for the resurgence in recent years of graphic signs in many parts of the country.

A rather special kind of sign with a wide variety of designs, was used by customers rather than tradesmen. This was the fire-mark, the small cast metal plate issued by the earliest insurance companies for display on the buildings which they would protect. The vagaries of the arrangements between the insurance companies and the volunteer fire brigades (unlike their English counterpart, the American fire insurance companies did not have their own fire brigades), were such that a building might not always get the protection its metal plate warranted, however. The first fire brigade to get to the scene of a fire had a right to the full reward the insurance company paid, unless the fire brigade called on another for help, which would have meant sharing the reward—a diminution of payment few were willing to accept. So a building might burn merrily away as the fire brigade struggling against it stubbornly refused to call for the help of the two or three others that could have saved it. The building might also burn while two companies arriving

115. Sheet tin weathervane of a horse thought to have been made in Michigan about the middle of the 19th century, and obviously used for target practice.

116. Gilt copper horse and sulky by an unknown 19th-century maker.

117. Wrought iron weathervane probably made in the late 18th century, once obviously the target of not a few local shots, now at the entrance to Yale University Art Gallery's American Wing, called 'American Arts and the American Experience'. Yale University Art Gallery, New Haven, Connecticut.

together settled their rights with fisticuffs! If a burning building did not carry a fire-mark, the cold-blooded firemen simply turned tail and reported a false alarm. Paid fire departments began to take the place of the volunteers in the second half of the 19th century, and fire-marks consequently lost their function, although some insurance companies continued to issue plates purely for advertising purposes.

A hitching post was a mark of class outside any store. The first were made of wood, and then iron—wrought and cast—became the most popular material.

The gaudiest and most flamboyant wood carvings of the latter part of the 19th century are found among the publicity figures on circus-wagons and the various creatures used for carrousels or merry-go-rounds, which, together with the later circus posters, combine what one observer calls . . . 'a mixture of ballyhoo and art'. Something of the flavour of the circus parade—what Ringling called the 'winding, dazzling river of silver and gold' and Barnum & Bailey dubbed 'The Greatest Show on Earth', is captured in miniature in the Circus Parade Building at the Shelburne Museum. Here you can wander past a scale model more than 500 feet long, of sixty Lilliputian band wagons, cage wagons, tableaux of one sort and another, animals, riders, clowns and musicians, the whole 'Dazzling, dancing scene in the Magical, Mighty, wordless play, combining the weird wizardry of India and Arabia in opulent oriental grandeur'.

Not much is known about the individual carvers, although some work has been attributed to Samuel Robb of New York, a known ship's carver who worked for the Sebastian Wagon Company, which specialised in circus and menagerie wagons and the embellishment thereof. A good deal of the work was certainly done in the Mid-West, particularly in Wisconsin, where for many years circuses had their winter quarters. Some of the best roundabout figures are said to have been made by Gustav Augustus Dentzel's factory in Germantown, Pennsylvania, in the 1890s. Many different kinds of birds and animals, real and imaginary, were made for the earliest carrousels, but it was soon discovered that most children preferred horses, especially the dapple-grey ones, apparently, and by the end of the century, horses had just about ousted all other creatures from the merry-go-round. I think that I might have enjoyed a ride on the giraffe which can be seen at the American Museum in Britain.

At one time or another, the first settlers along the Eastern seaboard and in the Mid-West had reason to be grateful that the largest bird migrations in the world take place up and down this continent. They also had reason to be grateful to the Indians, who many centuries earlier had devised a method, quickly adopted by the newcomers, of luring this food on the wing within shooting range, by judiciously

118. Oak whirligig probably made in Pennsylvania. The original is over 4 ft high. Toys with whirling arms have a long history in Europe. They seem to have been made as early as the middle of the 18th century in America and were probably used as wind indicators, scarecrows, or simply as garden decorations for the amusement of owners and passers-by. The name 'whirligig' used also to apply to round-abouts and merry-go-rounds. In New York in the early 19th century it was an 'exciting and dangerous' winter-sport, according to James Fenimore Cooper, a kind of snap-the-whip for sledge-riders.

119. Ship's figurehead at the entrance to the Colchester Reef Lighthouse at the Shelburne Museum, Vermont. Shelburne Museum, Vermont.

120. Fish weathervane thought to have been made in Rhode Island about 1890. One of the characters in James Fenimore Cooper's novel *The Pioneers*, set in Upper New York State early in the 19th century, has a fish weathervane atop his house, but 'although intended to answer the purpose of a weathercock, the fish was observed invariably to look with a longing eye in the direction of the beautiful sheet of water that lay imbedded in the mountains of Templeton'.

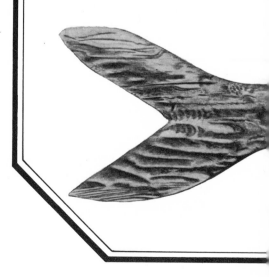

planting artificial birds along the shore, or in the marshes to, hand. These artificial birds came to be called 'coy'—from the Dutch word *kooi*, meaning cage or trap—which by some means, as yet undetermined, became 'decoy', as we know it today. The carving of these wooden creatures is said to have been perfected about the time of the Civil War in the 1860s, and is still done today much as it was then. Materials other than wood, such as cork, balsa, wood, tin and iron, used not to have quite the cachet that solid white pine and cedar have, but have been gaining in collector interest in recent years. Some people think that the numerous factory-made models are inferior in design to the hand-carved models, but others consider that certain of the factory decoys produced, by the Mason Company of Detroit, Michigan, for example, were so superior, that they were copied by many an individual craftsman.

There are basically two types of decoys: the stick-ups, and the floaters, which are found in the likenesses of every species of waterfowl hunted in this manner. Regional differences in the carving have been noted by Joel Barber, who wrote the first standard reference book on this subject in 1932. The best are considered to be those that suggest the essential characteristics of particular birds in the simplest, most stylised manner—most attractive to wild fowl as well as aesthetes, it seems! Those illustrated here are from the collection of the late William J. Mackey, a collector, scholar and connoisseur of the craft. They are all by early 20th-century carvers. Half of the Mackey collection of some 2,600 decoys was auctioned in Massachusetts in the summer of 1973, and the other half will be auctioned in 1974. Prices in the 1973 sales ranged from as low as $10 to as high as $10,500—not exactly the recession price which one collector expected from this flooding of the market.

Prices for weathervanes do not seem about to go into a recession. On the contrary, the frenzy to own a 19th-century weather indicator pushed the price of a gilded copper *Statue of Liberty* weathervane up to an incredible $26,000 in 1973. And in this case, it is the factory-made models which are reaching the record prices, because they are easier to identify than earlier examples that are readily faked and difficult to authenticate. Collectors are consequently poring over the catalogues of the large-scale manufacturers, such as J. W. Fiske, J. L. Mott and E. G. Washburne & Co. in the New York area and Cushing & White (later L. W. Cushing & Sons), J. Harris & Son and W. A. Snow in the Boston area, who in the latter part of the 19th century were turning out large numbers of weathervanes, mostly in sheet copper, which could be and were ordered from all parts of the country. There is some doubt as to whether all the designs found in the catalogues were ever made. Before sheet copper became the predominant material, wood, iron and tin, were used

121. Cigarstore Indian—scout type.

122. Cigarstore Indian—Pocahontas type, although belted dresses and high-buttoned shoes would not have been found on many, if any Indian women. (Pocahonatas, in case you have forgotten, was the daughter of an Indian chief who saved the life of the leader of the Jamestown settlers in Virginia early in the 17th century, married one of the other new arrivals and died of smallpox in London when she was still only eighteen or twenty years old.)

123. Two rare long-billed curlews from Mason's Decoy Factory, Detroit, Michigan. Since the Mason factory employed some of the finest wood-workers they had some basis for claiming to be the 'largest exclusive manufacturer of decoys in the world.' The long-billed or sickle-billed curlews are the largest of the largest shore-birds.

123

124a

123

124. Canada geese: rare early stick-up type (a) with cork body and white pine head from Long Island, New York and hollow-carved type (b) made in New Jersey. The Canada goose is widely distributed over North America but is unique to this hemisphere. It is the largest of the wildfowl family after the swan and the crane.

125

125. Canada goose: extremely rare hollow-carved sleeping type made by Sam Soper of New Jersey.

124b

separately and in various combinations. A very rare 18th-century pewter figure of Triton is in the Shelburne Museum, Vermont. The yellow ochre paint on some wooden vanes is thought to be the economical country cousin of the gold leaf occasionally used on metal vanes.

The most common pre-Revolutionary subjects were arrows and bannerets, cocks and Indians, although the most famous weathervane made by the earliest known professional maker, 'Deacon' Shem Drowne of Boston, is a hammered copper grasshopper, which is still in the spot for which it was made—the cupola of Faneuil Hall in Boston. Drowne got his inspiration in 1749 from the grasshopper atop the Royal Exchange in London, and both were in turn copied late in the 19th century by the Massachusetts company of L. W. Cushing & Sons.

In the 19th century, the choice of subject more often depended on local interest: cows and bulls and other livestock for farmers (according to one estimate, dairy cattle are the most popular of all, at least on barns and silos, according to another estimate, cocks and horses have it over all others); maritime subjects, in seacoast villages; other trades, hobbies and sports, a team of running horses drawing a hose wagon or pumper for a firestation; a locomotive for the railway station; a quill for scholars and journalists and other scribblers; and the continuing presence of the cock or rooster and other ecclesiastical symbols, such as the archangel Gabriel or a fish, on churches. The horse which probably inspired the most weathervanes, was a Vermont trotter by the name of Ethan Allen (named after one of the State's Revolutionary War heroes), which was reputed to be the fastest trotter in the nation in the 1850s. Human figures are relatively rare, possibly because they are difficult to do. Other rare and unusual subjects are serpents and dragons, Mercury and Diana, an owl and a pussycat. That gadget-lover, President Thomas Jefferson, had a shaft installed in his home at Monticello, Virginia, leading down from the weathervane on the roof to an indicator in the ceiling in the room below, so that he did not have to go outdoors to find out what the wind was doing!

The spate of weathervane thefts in recent years, by nimble-footed ladder-climbers or even helicopter-borne thieves, as well as the sky-rocketing of prices, has led owners to take a variety of precautions to safeguard their treasures. They photograph them and stamp them with identifying marks. And they keep the bill-of-sale in a safe place, not only for identification, but to ensure the return of the purchase price in case their vane turns out to be stolen property. Knowing how many shotgun holes are in your vane, or how many points there are in your rooster's comb, also helps to identify it.

126 & 127. Toy animals made by the Pennsylvanian woodcarver, Wilhelm Schimmel. Titus C. Geesey Collection, Philadelphia Museum of Art, Pennsylvania.

The landbased whittlers and carvers had their naval counterparts in the skrimshanderers, to coin a word, the sailors who passed their time, during long whaling and other voyages, making useful and decorative objects to take back home or use on board ship. All of these objects which are made out of whalebone and the ivory teeth of sperm whales and are etched or incised with a variety of designs, have come to be known as scrimshaw. The origin of the word seems to be somewhat obscure. It may well have something to do with 'scrimshank', an old military slang word of equally obscure origin, meaning a shirker. Some believe the origin is a Dutch word for a lazy fellow, and it is not inconceivable that shipboard whittlers were so considered. The Smithsonian Institution, on the other hand, suggests that the word has more to do with 'fussy workmanship'. And when you think about it, these two interpretations are not necessarily mutually exclusive, especially considering the painstaking and time-consuming nature of the task the scrimshanderers had given themselves.

Elephant and walrus tusks, cow and oxen horns, have

been carved for centuries and used for such objects as powder horns, on which hunter and soldier alike lavished great care during the 17th and 18th centuries. Just when New England whalemen began their whittling with whalebone and the teeth of sperm whales–the art considered peculiar to them–is not clear, but possibly they got the idea from the Normandy ivory workers they came in contact with, after their ships began using Dunkirk as a whaling port, late in the 18th century.

The basic tool for scrimshaw was a jack-knife, but needles were also needed for scraping and prizing out the designs, and awls, files and gimlets for boring holes and piercing–all the 'dentistical looking instruments specially intended for the skrimshandering business' which, as Herman Melville noted in his whaling story, *Moby Dick*, many sailors carried about with them in little boxes.

The most famous pieces of scrimshaw are the teeth etched with ships and whales, foreign ports and other marine studies, as well as portraits of women. Such subjects were frequently taken from a book or magazine, pasted on to a tooth and then scratched through. Indian ink, and coloured inks on the more ambitious pieces, lamp-black, tar or paint, was then applied. Crimping or jagging wheels for running a decorative edge around a pie, and busks or bodice stays from whalebone, were popular pieces to take home, and so were a variety of other objects such as swifts for winding yarn or wool, clothespins and rolling pins, napkin rings and knitting needles, wick-pickers for oil lamps, baskets and canes. For their own use the whalemen made various small pieces of equipment such as yardsticks and fids, oil-cask measures and blocks and cleats for the sail and mast, as well as cribbage boards and checkers and chess sets and scrimshaw needle-boxes.

Separated by over a thousand miles of prairie and desert from the main thrust of the European settlement of America coming from the east, were the isolated northern frontiers of Spanish penetration from the south west. And it was there–in what is now mainly the States of New Mexico and Arizona–that during the late 18th and early 19th centuries a distinctive style of religious carving and painting was developed by priests, and another band of itinerant and largely anonymous craftsmen, the *santeros*, or makers of saints, or more precisely of the carved and painted likenesses of saints. These were of two types–the *bultos*, or carved figures in the round, and the *retablos*, or flat painted panels–and were used in churches and homes. They were made from local materials such as pine and cottonwood roots, gesso made from gypsum, and mineral and vegetable pigments. Two pigments imported from Mexico–indigo and cochineal–were also used. One figure, that of Saint Rita of Cascia, the Patroness of the Impossible, would surely be a comfort on any frontier.

128. Butt and lock of a Pennsylvanian long rifle made by Jacob Dickert of Lancaster, Pennsylvania, about 1775–80.

129. Cast iron fire-mark painted to resemble bronze.

130. Cast iron fire-mark of the Fire Department Insurance Company, Cincinnati, Ohio about 1850.

131. (page 126) Bread and butter Americana–the iron wall in Yale University Art Gallery's American Wing, now called 'American Arts and the American Experience'. In defiance of British restrictive legislation, the American Colonists built up a considerable iron industry in the 18th century–without it the revolutionary armies might not have done as well as they did. Most of the pieces here are roughly dated late 18th century or 19th century. The skewers are modern and the locks German–'made for the American market'. The adjustable cross-arm on the candlestand is thought to be peculiarly American. The long rifle was streamlined and perfected by Pennsylvania craftsmen working on the edge of the frontier around the middle of the 18th century into the deadliest weapon of its time. The halberd–that's a halberd head above the gun–once used as a weapon was more often carried by state guards, sergeants-at-arms, sometimes even church beadles on ceremonious occasions in New England until quite recent times.

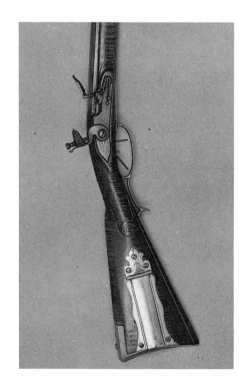

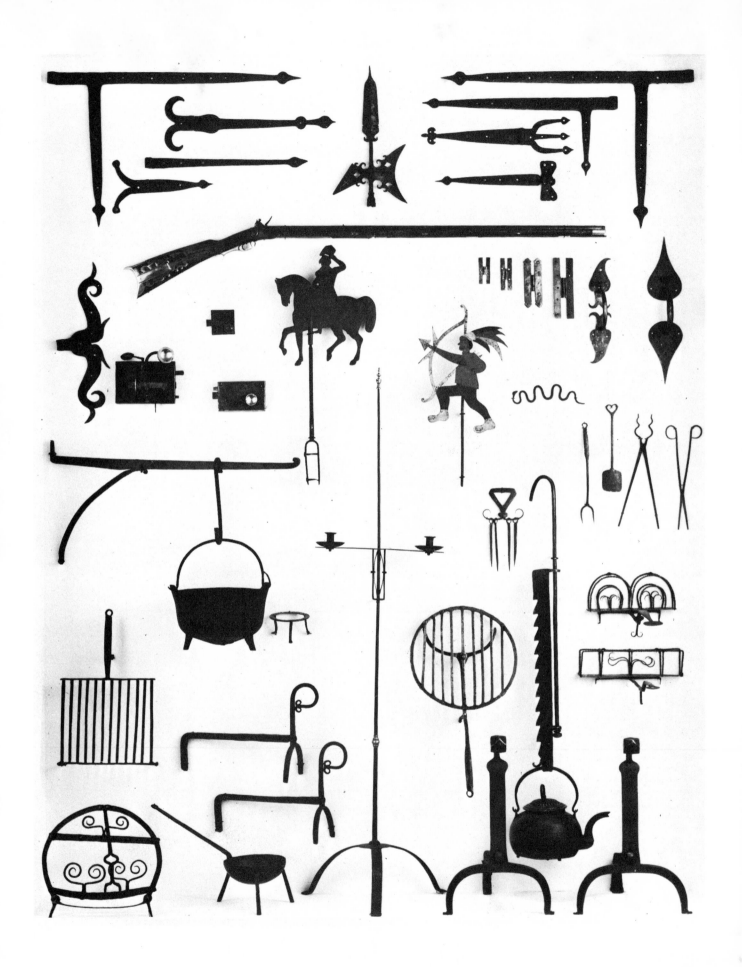